Ever So Grateful!

*Poetic Praise and Thankgiving
to My Most Beloved*

BEVERLY RILEY GRAVES

ISBN 978-1-956896-11-4 (softcover)
ISBN 978-1-956896-12-1 (hardcover)
ISBN 978-1-956896-13-8 (ebook)

Printed in the United States of America.

Book Vine Press
2516 Highland Dr.
Palatine, IL 60067

Dedication

In loving memory of

Juanita "Neet" McClendon

You have touched and enriched so many lives.
I am *ever so grateful* one of them was mine!

Missing you dearly, Mom.
Until we meet again
—*Brat*

For the Lord Himself shall descend from Heaven with a shout, with the voice of the Archangel, and with the trump of God: and the dead in Christ shall rise first: Then we which are alive and remain shall be caught up together with them in the clouds, to meet the Lord in the air: and so shall we ever be with the Lord. (1 Thessalonians 4:16–17, KJV)

Acknowledgements

To my wonderful husband and best friend, Benjamin, for your support and patience during the process of putting this book together. Although I spent many hours writing and editing, you never once complained. I especially appreciate your many prayers, asking God to bless this book and allow it to be a blessing to others.
Thank you, sweetheart. I love you so much!

To my mother, Thelma V. Riley, for giving me my first glimpse of the wonderful love of God. Your strength and courage continue to inspire me.
Without you, this book would not have been possible.

To my sister, Delores Francois, for always being there to hear my countless first drafts over and over again. Thank you so much for your listening ear, encouraging words and generosity of heart.

To Pastor Rodney Grissom and the Emmanuel Temple Church Family for allowing me to share my poetic testimonies of God's love and faithfulness. I thank you for your prayers, your spiritual guidance and your many kind words of encouragement.

To my children, grandchildren and great-grandchildren for loving me in spite of myself. The past year has been very tough on our "family get-togethers," but God continues to be ever so gracious. I pray the light of His love will permeate your hearts and minds and His peace will be yours for always.

And finally, to my grand-dog, Buddy, for smothering me with affection! He has taught me a lot about God's unconditional love, and we are most grateful for the special joy he has brought into our lives.

Contents

Praise and Thanksgiving

Faith and Trust

Peace and Comfort

Caring and Sharing

Family and Friends

Final Praise

Preface

Some years ago, I came across a beautiful poem written by George Herbert (1593–1633) entitled "Gratefulness." This truly aspiring poem is a poignant prayer, petitioning the Lord for a grateful heart. I was especially moved by the words so fervently quoted below:

Thou that hast given so much to me
Give one thing more, a grateful heart:
Not thankful when it pleaseth me...
But such a heart whose pulse may be Thy praise.

My heart was deeply touched! I decided right then to make the sentiments of this prayer my own. And so I promptly typed up the verse, placed it in a clear, protective sheet and displayed it on my desk—and there it remained for almost twenty years. Just a few weeks before my retirement, I thoughtfully read the verse again, as I have done so many times before. But this time, I suddenly realized that God has been answering this prayer throughout these many years. He has graciously given favor to my request, even before I asked and despite the fact it sometimes went unnoticed on my desk. Yes, God, who "hast given so much to me," had given me one thing more—a grateful heart.

I believe the precious gift of "gratefulness" never ends but is ever ascending upwards and outwards; and lest, through my own negligence, it be taken away, I claimed yet another verse of George Herbert's prayer, which continues to be my beggarly plea:

Wherefore I cry, and cry again
And in no quiet canst Thou be
Till I a thankful heart obtain of Thee

The poems in this book has been written from a heart that is ever so grateful to God for His lovingkindness and mercies. He has carried me through many dreadful storms; but every pain, every tear and every heartache has brought me closer to Him in indebted love and gratitude. Oh, I am beholden to the Most High God of Israel and will be for all eternity! Thus, throughout the pages of this book, you will find offerings of thanksgiving and praise unto My Sweet and Most Beloved who has made my heart *abundantly* full with His goodness and who has set me before His presence forever!

O Thou for whom my soul adores
Bind me in weighted chains of gold
That I may ne'er escape Thy love
But upon Thy loveliness behold
Thou art My Sweet and Most Beloved
Who hast made my heart supremely full
Thus I, alone, remain of men...
Most blest and ever so grateful!

—Beverly Riley Graves

Prayer

and

Deliverance

FLY SWIFTLY, MY ANGEL • HE KNOWS MY STORM • HE SENDS AN ANGEL
HIS NAME IS DELIVERANCE • HIS THRONE OF GRACE
IT IS GOOD TO HAVE BEEN AFFLICTED • IT WAS A STORM
RESCUED! • THE ENEMY IS HERE • THIS TRYING HOUR
THOU HAST TAUGHT US TO PRAY • THOU THAT SAVETH • UNSEEN

What an awesome privilege it is to kneel before the Majesty of Heaven in prayer! It is heartening to know He is interested in our day-to-day activities and challenges, and He is ever interceding and intervening on our behalf. Each and every time I cried out to our gracious Father, He heard my voice from Heaven and turned His face towards me. I can truly say, as did King David, "The Lord is my rock, and my fortress, and my deliverer. He delivered me from my strong enemy, and from them that hated me" (2 Samuel 22:2, 18, KJV). And thus, from the depths of my heart and with the utmost love and gratitude, I attest to His great and wonderful name—for His name is Deliverance!

Fly Swiftly, My Angel

Are not the angels all ministering spirits (servants) sent out in the service [of God for the assistance] of those who are to inherit salvation?
—Hebrews 1:14 (AMPC)

Fly swiftly, my Angel
On thy wings, bear my prayers
Unto the bosom of Jesus
For He's awaiting me there
In His chambers of mercy
At the Throne of His Grace
May my prayers ascend softly
Ne'er an utterance escape
Till He bends His head slightly
At the sound of my cries
And gives ear to my groanings
For I need Him just now
So Angel excelling
In strength and in might
Draw full of His riches
Then return to thy flight
Make haste thou dear guardian
Bearing gifts on thy wings
Sweet abundance of blessings
From the heart of my King

Then, Angel, stay near me
As my lips sing His praise
Waft your wings greatly
Keep the dark clouds away
For my spirit rejoices
My Father hast favored me
Valiant celestial beings
He sent to deliver me

Sweet messengers of God
Encamping all around
Hast made this lowly place
Indeed now sacred ground
Armies of Heaven's Light
Hast led to victory
O Prince what shall I give
For what Thou hast done for me

O heart in reverence bow
Such praise can't be contained
His love that knows no bounds
Hast lifted my poor soul again
So, Angel, guard my words
Hold captive every one
Take thou my utmost thanks
Back to my Father's Throne
Here I shall prostrate lie
As thou my offering bring
Release my grateful breath
Beneath thy fluttering wings
Till He, whose clothed in light
Inhales my deepest praise
And gives His tenderest thought
To one He died to save
That I, myself, some day may bow
Upon His nail-scarred feet
And there my joyful tears of praise
Shall forever bathe eternity

O Angel, thou must swiftly fly
Bear my love upon thy wings
Till thou hast laid my grateful heart
Upon the sweet bosom of my King

March 30, 2015

(Dedicated to Janice Moore)

Behold, I send an Angel before thee, to keep thee in the way, and to bring thee into the place which I have prepared. (Exodus 23:20, KJV)

He Knows My Storm

When the poor and needy seek water, and there is none, and their tongue faileth for thirst, I the Lord will hear them, I the God of Israel will not forsake them. I will open rivers in high places, and fountains in the midst of the valleys: I will make the wilderness a pool of water, and the dry land springs of water. That they may see, and know, and consider, and understand together, that the hand of the Lord hath done this, and the Holy One of Israel hath created it.
—Isaiah 41:17–18, 20 (KJV)

Apart from Thee, O Lord, I languish
in a dry and thirsty land
Apart from Thee, my lips are parched
my vocal chords are strained
There is no water or cooling shade
and thus my voice hast lost her praise
I wither, I die; no breath or life
as fading, scattering, brittle leaves
in the blowing winds of time

I come to Thee fainthearted, Lord
timid and afraid—
haunted by my troubled past
disheartened by the evils of this day
while the dark unknowns of tomorrow lie in wait
and I cannot break these heavy chains
I'm too frail to rise above my pain
while missing so my heavenly home
and Thee

Yet, time and time again
I hear Thy voice
piercing the shadows of darkness
Thine ever-tender, seeking heart
reaches out to me—

Thy love awakens love
and the yearnings of my wanting heart
follows after Thee
for Thou, and Thou alone, can comfort me
and though I've lost my words, my voice
whether by happenstance or choice
it is God who speaks
it is God who pours *Himself*
all over me

Lord, Thou knows my storm
and my storm knows Thee
for Thou wouldst hold my trembling form
firmly to Thy breast
till the tempest, squalls of frightful night
is stilled and quieted
and I, in utter gratefulness
know treasured peace and rest
In Thee, my thirsty soul is quenched
and blessed!

Yes Lord, Thou knows well *this* storm
and this storm knows *all* of Thee
for it shutters when my trusting heart
lifts up her wearied eyes—beyond Earth's skies
and entering into Thy dwelling place
I find a shelter, warm and safe
a mighty fortress, vast and strong
impervious to the likes of storms
and anchored deep in Everlasting arms—
arms wide opened just for me

O again and again and again
I hear the sweetness of Thy voice
reminding me of such steadfast love
that does not e'er forsake
and in awe of Thy great faithfulness
beneath the winds of Thy mighty wings...
I rise; I soar—
so brave and unafraid
no longer in that desert place
for *Thou art God*
and I am surely known of Thee

O Thou hast raised my voice, O Lord!
Thou hast raised my voice in praise!
with words and verse and joyful songs—
sweet offerings unto Thy Gracious Name!

O Thou hast opened up my lips
and my tongue resonates Thy praise
for my soul hast been made satisfied
I've been refreshed, renewed, revitalized
plunged beneath the mighty, gushing waters
The Fountain of Life—
ah, the luscious wellsprings
of His Grace!

I lift my voice unto Thee, My Lord
I lift up my voice in praise!

October 19, 2020

O God, Thou art my God; early will I seek Thee: my soul thirsteth for Thee,
my flesh longeth for Thee in a dry and thirsty land. (Psalm 63:1, KJV)

O Lord, open Thou my lips; and my mouth shall shew forth Thy praise.
(Psalm 51:15, KJV)

My soul shall be satisfied as with marrow and fatness; and
my mouth shall praise Thee with joyful lips.
(Psalm 63:5, KJV)

He Sends an Angel

And when he came to the den... the king spake and said to Daniel, O Daniel, servant of the living God, is thy God, whom thou servest continually, able to deliver thee from the lions? Then said Daniel unto the king, O king, live forever. My God hath sent His angel, and hath shut the lions' mouths. —Daniel 6:20–22 (KJV)

"My God hath sent His angel
And hath shut the lions' mouths"
And I no longer am a prey
To be torn and tossed about
For He hast graciously delivered
And hast gone beyond all means
To protect His child in danger
From an enemy shrewd and keen

"My God hath sent His angel"
Who takes me by the hand
And hurries me to safety
Out of a doomed and wicked land
He places me where my steps are sure
Far from destruction's way
He is a kind and gentle Father
With eyes that searches out to save

And Christ, Himself, the Archangel
Into the fiery furnace He came
The Son of God, my covering
From a hot and burning flame
In His presence, fire loses its power
Kings and kingdoms are brought low
For the humble prayer of His trusting child
He speaks—and it is so!

Make no mistake, He delivers well
He delivers strong indeed
What love! I cannot understand
What love to such as me!
That when the foe would cast me out
Into the darkest night
With haste, He sends His angel
For we are precious in His sight

And He will always send His angel
Ten thousands if need be
For He, The Great Commander
Fights the battles for you and me
Our confidence in Him is sure
For His love removes all doubt
My God will send His angel
And He will shut the lions' mouths!

January 24, 2012

(To Elaina)

His Name Is Deliverance

But Thou art holy, O Thou that inhabitest the praises of Israel. Our fathers trusted in Thee: they trusted, and Thou didst deliver them. They cried unto Thee, and were delivered. —Psalm 22:3–5 (KJV)

Thou Lord, whose name is Savior
Thou Lord, whose name is Deliverer
Bend now Thine ear to the voice of this penitent
Rescue my soul from the eye of the pestilence
Helpless, I fall on bended knees
Daunting these chains I raise to Thee...
"O Thou that inhabitest the praises of Israel"
Come quickly that I may of Thy mercies avail
Instruct Thou the path of this turbulent sea
Contend now with those that contendeth with me
O Lord, I pray for deliverance...

For Thou, Lord, doth search the hearts of Thy children
Their desires ascend to the seat of Thy Throne
Hitherto our fathers have trusted in Thee
And were delivered by the strength of Thine infinite arms
Thou doth faithfully order the steps of Thy people
Unceasingly bending from Thy chambers on high
With each whisper, each groan, each questioning brow
Thou doth answer, "I am here! It is I!"

Thou Lord, whose name is Almighty
Thou Lord, whose name is Everlasting
Destroy now this audacious stronghold of the enemy
Lend me Thy power; I am exceedingly weak
For my strength is dried up
My bones are as dust
But Thou who hast been The Lifter Up of my head
O Thou who art still the Sweet Balm of Gilead

Regard me once more, and give ear to my plea
Break asunder these bars that I may be free
O Lord, I pray for deliverance

O Thou who reserves the forces of nature
The thunder, the lightning, the hail and the rain
And commandeth the storm to be silent before Thee
And it humbly obeys and bows down to Thy name
Thou doth gracefully fly on the wings of the morning
Reconstructing the path of the infamous wind
And beckons its breath to lay waste to the wicked
While restoring my soul again and again
O Thou who hast fathered the earth and the heavens
And doth master the waves of the billowing seas
Divide now the waters on behalf of Thy servant
And attend to the cry that reaches even unto Thee

The Lord God, who is ever "merciful and gracious
Longsuffering, and abundant in goodness and truth
Keeping mercy for thousands," yea thousands upon thousands
Not only forgives, but cleanses us too
O come, Blest Redeemer! Thou art mighty to save!
Deliver me just now from the sword and the grave
And I shall declare forever Thy name
That Thou, through eternity, may delight in my praise

O Thou, who inhabits the praises of Thy children
O Thou, who abides in the praises of Thy children
O Thou, who delights in the praises of Thy children...
Beneath Thy sure wings I shall hide
Till Thou hast made my poor soul satisfied

I pray for deliverance
Thy name is Deliverance!
Thy name is Deliverance!
Everlasting Deliverer!
Make haste, God Almighty, for me!
Make haste, Thou Blessed Savior, for me!

March 23, 2018

And the Lord passed by before him, and proclaimed,
The Lord, The Lord God, merciful and gracious, longsuffering,
and abundant in goodness and truth, keeping mercy for thousands,
forgiving iniquity and transgression and sin. (Exodus 34:6–7, KJV)

His Throne of Grace

Let us therefore come boldly unto the throne of grace, that we may obtain mercy, and find grace to help in time of need. —Hebrews 4:16 (KJV)

There are times when the clouds of life have dimmed my view
And the warming light of sunshine just isn't getting through
The sweet joy that filled my life
Has been emptied; I'm not sure why
But my soul dost yearn to see His face
So I hasten to that sacred place
Where I lay down all my pains and aches before His Throne of Grace

There are moments when my burdened soul lays open, bare
And the heavy weight of sinfulness drives me to despair
For indeed I am unworthy; I am utterly undone
How can I, so great a sinner, approach the Holy One
But it seems I just can't stay away
And though I don't know what to say
My guilty heart falls helplessly before His Throne of Grace

And O how sweet and graciously my Father attends to me
With gentle loving tenderness, He satisfies my needs
For truly He is the Bread of Life
The Living Water; and I am revived
For His Fountain ever flows
It is for the healing of our souls
And praise His name I can now lay claim to *all* blessings He bestows

O weary soul when it seems the world is just too much to bear
God has given us the privilege to come to Him in prayer
Like precious holy incense our fervent prayers will rise
A sweet and fragrant savor before our Father's eyes
So let us give to Him an offering
On the altar lay our everything
As we humbly bow before our King at this most favored place

"Let us therefore come boldly unto the Throne of Grace
That we may obtain mercy" as we seek our Father's face
And find grace to help in the time of need
And a light to guide our wayward feet
He's the balm of Gilead for our pain
For our thirsty hearts, abundant rain
In Him our stormy seas are stilled
As the foe gives way to the Master's will
God will move mountains; He will open doors
And His Holy Spirit, He shall fully outpour

For the Lord is our Redeemer, The Holy and Reverend
The Lord God Almighty, His name alone is Excellent
For the Lord is our Shepherd, The Lord our Righteousness
A name for all our needs whereby His children shall be blessed
He shall be called Wonderful, Counselor, the Mighty God, the Prince of Peace
He shall reign on the Throne of David, and His kingdom shall never cease
Jehovah Shalom, Jehovah Rapha, Jehovah Nissi, Jehovah Jireh
Our Perfect Peace, our Blessed Healer, our Victory Banner, our Supreme Provider
O bless His Name for His arms are full of goodness and sure mercies
For there is no other name whereby a sinner is made free

You see... the Most High God is whom we seek when we kneel to pray
And He's awaiting *even me* at His Sweet Throne of Grace
Where His exceedingly abundant riches fill my every need
As I cast my dying soul before His mercy seat
Praise, awe and adoration then floods my lifted soul
For the Precious Lamb of God this day has made me whole

Yes, the Merciful God is able; the Compassionate will sustain
Who was and is and forever shall be
For Jehovah *is* His name!

March 17, 2013

(Dedicated to Sis. Mary Willis)

It Is Good to Have Been Afflicted

It is good for me that I have been afflicted; that I might learn Thy statutes.
—Psalm 119:71 (KJV)

I recall the deeply troubled nights
The pains of heart were strong
The morning seemed so far away
And I was left alone
A victim of a shattered heart
With pieces thrown about
And none could see the brokenness
Or hear my screams and shouts

But it was good to have been afflicted
Or else how would I've known
The tender mercies of a loving God
To whom my heart belongs
He plucked me up from the grasp of hell
And held me to His breast
In a moment, storms were silenced
And my heart was brought to rest
Yes, it was good to have been afflicted
For who but God can save
And who like God can deliver one
From a dark and certain grave
Who other than the Prince of Peace
Can soothe the trembling soul
And who but the great Physician
Can make the broken whole

At times the road we take is hard
And we just can't understand
The hows, the whys, what brought us here
To where all is sinking sand

In times like these, He still is God
And you are yet His child
Have faith, our Father never fails
He will bring you through *this* trial
And O how God delivers
As only a Savior could
He is worthy of our highest praise
For His afflictions are for good

Yes, it is good to have been afflicted
For when our sorrows come
He may not take the pain away
But He brings us through each one
For when life bears hard upon us
God makes His presence known
And His deliverance shall be mighty
For He is most gracious to His own
Thus, afflictions cannot crush the soul
Who waits beneath His care
For God in His great gentleness
Gives no more than we can bear

Yes, it is good to have been afflicted
For it draws my eyes above
And keeps me firmly in the sheltering arms
Of His great and awesome love

November 19, 2011

(Dedicated, with fondest memories, to a special mother, Juanita McClendon)

It Was a Storm

In my distress I called upon the Lord, and cried to my God: and He did hear my voice out of His temple, and my cry did enter into His ears.
—2 Samuel 22:7 (KJV)

It was a storm that brought me here
Safe in the shelter of His care
The storm that caused such bitter pain
And poured with wrath torrential rains
The violent, angry, raging seas
With every wave engulfing me
The thunderous sound of evil voice
The cries, the screams, the deafening noise
And I fell helpless in the hands
Of he who delights in wicked plans
Who seeks such joy in man's demise
Through shrewd and cunning, deceitful lies
'Twas such a storm and O how great
Yet for that storm, I give Him praise

It was a storm that brought me here
Unto the Lord I now hold dear
The mighty waves with ebb and flow
That pushed and pulled with highs and lows
And left my soul to drown in night
All drained of strength from bitter fight
It even seems love turns its head
From those whose tears would flood their beds
Who lie awake with anxious minds
All void of hope for better times
And death itself sometimes seems sweet
When pains of life can't be relieved
'Twas such a storm and O how great
But for that storm, I give Him praise

For when my eyes searched out the skies
I saw the gleamer of a silver line
My Father's hands stretched out to me
Extending far beyond dark seas
Though I had turned against His will
His saving hands were reaching still
His reaching hands were saving still
With astounding love my heart to fill
Such love that would not let me go
Brought comfort to my anguished soul
For He rode the winds of storms to free
That grip that darkness had on me
The mighty God whose clothed in light
Dispels the power of the blackest night
And darkness cowers beneath His words
And flees the presence of my Lord

Then with sweet inhaling of His breath
He raises me unto Himself
And rocks me in His gentle arms
With tender song to soothe and calm
For the Mighty God stands by my side
My Rock, my Tower, my Friend and Guide
My Beloved who holds with massive arms
That carries me through every storm
And thus my soul has found true rest
As He does all things for my best

Yes, it was my God who brought me here
By way of storms, He draws us near
And teaches us to trust His hand
That we through trials may firmly stand
For the Strength of Israel is at our side
More so when by fire our souls are tried

For we are privileged to *boldly* approach His Throne
Where the Most High waits to show Himself strong
There... to bask in the gift of His marvelous grace
There... to receive of His strength for the battles we face
Holdfast, for He that shall come, will come
And will take us away to our heavenly home
Then all of life's trials will seem pale when compared
To life everlasting in the home He's prepared
O to live in the presence of the Christ we adore
O to gaze on His face and give praise evermore
O to know blissful rest in the Infinite's arms
O to be at that place where there are no storms

Very soon... there will be no more storms!
Very soon... there will be no more storms!

October 22, 2013

(To my daughter, Alisha)

And I heard a great voice out of Heaven saying, Behold, the tabernacle of God is with men, and He will dwell with them, and they shall be His people and God Himself shall be with them, and be their God. And God shall wipe away all tears from their eyes; and there shall be no more death, neither sorrow, nor crying, neither shall there be any more pain: for the former things are passed away. (Revelations 21:3–4, KJV)

Rescued!

The angel of the Lord encampeth round about them that fear Him, and delivereth them. —Psalm 34:7 (KJV)

Here I am Lord...
In that place where my heart doth fear to go
In the dark, in the deep, in the bitter cold
Confused and hurt that my prayer was seemingly ignored
When I would ask for sunshine, Thou, instead, hast sent a storm?
Doth not Thine ear bend most tenderly unto Thine own?
Why hast Thou left me here so helpless and utterly alone?
Yet, although the light of day my eyes doth fail to see
And I cannot understand Thy works, my faith looks *still* to Thee

Then Thou sendeth out Thine angel that I might see Thy face
Then another, and another till I'm warmed with Thine embrace
And I'm reminded: I am just mere man and knoweth not Thy ways
And I, ashamed, fall at Thy feet, so unworthy of Thy grace
But beg that Thou would keep my steps in Thy kind, omniscient hands
And make me slow to question what I cannot fully comprehend
For Thou hast rescued me—in spite of me—and hath made my eyes to see
That Thy grace *is* sufficient and saves with might one such as me!

And thus my heart is lifted in such praise that hitherto hast been unknown
For The Sweet Majesty of Heaven still sits high upon His Throne
And hast made perfect my affliction, carrying me higher than before
To the very gates of Heaven, unto the One my heart adores
O His eyes are always watchful and His presence ever near
When the foe would make me tremble, God erases every fear
For He saves with everlasting arms and delivers wholly out of night
And makes this lowly soul to bask in the warmth of Heaven's light

So here I am Lord...
Please forgive this lack of faith that made my heart to question Thine
Engrave these Thy words upon my heart: "Fear not, thou art Mine"

That I may rest beneath Thy care when sight hast failed these weary eyes
For *Thou alone* presides all-knowing over Earth, the seas, the skies
And with a heart that Thou hast humbled, my soul bends in deference Lord to Thee
For without the storm, this I would not know: Thou saveth still... *miraculously!*

And now the day is ended; Thou hast brought me safely home
Thou *didst* answer well my anxious prayer with heart tender to Thine own
And when Earth's woeful night hast ended, and I no more amiss shall long
Thou shall grant, at last, my heart's desire when with Thee, I am at home

Thou shall grant, O Lord, my heart's desire, for with Thee, I will be home

January 14, 2017

The Enemy is Here

Ye are of God, little children, and have overcome them: because greater is He that is in you, than he that is in the world. —1 John 4:4 (KJV)

The enemy is here
I can feel a weighted cloud upon my brow
I can hear his whisperings, cruel and foul
And the fearful sounds of iron shackles
Amid the dark and ghastly shadows
That quickly hide the brightness of the day
And cause me to grope in blackness and lose my way

The enemy is here
For the air grows stagnate, stale and cold
And I grow swiftly faint beneath this strangely heavy load
The constant pitter-patter of unrelenting strife
The cruelty of words, the viciousness of life
I long to find a place where I can hide
A place where the enemy cannot abide
And as I search the distant skies to find my Father's face
I wonder why He has left me in this most distressing place

But in His time
I can feel the gentle squeeze of a loving Father's hand
And I can scarcely make my mind to fully comprehend
Could it be that He was here beside me all the time?
Can the night display such power as to make the heart go blind?
Yes, it is true that apart from Him there is no light of day
And thus my soul must cling to Him till He takes the clouds away
And though at times it seems that He is slow to heed my prayer
When His vengeance is awakened, it is terrible to bear

For in the deep of this fearful night where grisly shadows fall
He hears the voice of His trusting child and gives favor to her call

He answers out of the whirlwind, as the thunder sounds His voice
He wields His spear as lightning, striking all whom He appoints
And none can stand against the might of His great and awful hands
And the cruel, dark doings of the evil one disperse at His command
And I am yet amazed again that He does this all for me
O there is no love like my Most Beloved in whom *no* power can defeat

And as I walk away, leaning on the One who gave His all for me
I'm assured that He who loves me most is *far greater* than my enemy
And all who rest beneath the wings of His encompassing care
Can take courage, He will never give us more than we can bear
For in the mightiest storms of life and the fiercest tempest wild
He emerges still as the King of Kings, and even more... I am His child
Thus, it matters not what powerful weapons this formidable foe may hurl
For greater is He that is in me than he that is in the world!

September 5, 2014

(Dedicated to Debra Southern)

This Trying Hour

The name of the Lord is a strong tower: the righteous runneth into it, and is safe. —Proverbs 18:10 (KJV)

Lord, Thou art my strength
My safe and strong tower
I look to Thee alone
Expecting power
As weakness swallows me
My eyes are fixed on Thee
Be Thou my Mighty God
This trying hour

The tempter overwhelms the night
With darkness bold
The storm is fierce and swift
I sink beneath its load
If Thou but hold my hand
I know that I can stand
In spite of stormy sea
And bitter cold

Because God walks with me
The tempter loses his power
My strength hast been renewed
This trying hour
What help is there, but Thine?
What joy can equal mine?
Because I trust in Thee
Thou rescued me

For love that shelters me
I praise Thee, Lord
This soul's delight Thou art
My shield and sword

My affliction hast been blest
Herein my heart shall rest
Leaning always on Thy breast
My steps are sure

October 3, 2011

For Thou hast been a shelter for me, and a strong tower from the enemy. (Psalm 61:3, KJV)

Thou Hast Taught Us To Pray

*The Lord thundered from Heaven, and the Most High uttered His voice.
And He sent out arrows, and scattered them; lightning, and discomfited
them. He sent from above, He took me; He drew me out of many waters;
He delivered me from my strong enemy, and from them that hated me.
—2 Samuel 22:14–15, 17–18 (KJV)*

*Behold, the Lord's hand is not shortened, that it cannot save; neither His
ear heavy, that it cannot hear. —Isaiah 59:1 (KJV)*

Sometimes evil forces fall upon us without end
It seems the trying battles are near impossible to win
For the arrows just keep coming, and the pain is hard to bear
And the promise of a better day doesn't seem to ease my cares
But suddenly I'm reminded by a Beloved and Precious Friend
That He, who has my beginning, He too has my end
And He hast gifted *me* the privilege to approach His Throne of Grace
For God, in His great wisdom, hast taught me how to pray

The fervent prayer is ushered safe upon the wings of His love
Soaring higher, and yet higher still, to His dwelling place above
Where angels whisper softly, "Thy redemption draweth nigh"
As the light of Heaven pierces through the gross darkness of the night
For faith's request escapes the dross, finding access to His Throne
Where the Father's bended ear awaits the cries of His own
And *never* without His notice but with affectionate regard
His children's expectations fall upon His own heart
For Thou, who art Gracious, hath made a way of escape
When with all-excellent foresight, Thou did teach us to pray

I see Thine eyes like fire exacting judgements on those
Who disregard Thy law and would Thy children oppose
For they devise and conspire in the deep dark cover of night
Not knowing that God seeth still... in darkness as in light

Thou then utter Thy voice as thunder; the enemy scatters from sight
Thy hand then flashes as lightning, shooting arrows from on high
Thine eyes of love search far and low to the yearnings of Thy child
For he that touches her hath touched the apple of Thine eye
Heaven roars! The earth quakes! Thou obstructs the path of the angry sea!
Then, delivers her out of deep waters and raises her forthwith unto Thee
And how the heart erupts in praise and O what glorious strains
For the Most High God hath proven again and again and again
That His hand is not shortened; He is neither deaf that He cannot hear
For it was *my* cries that pierced the ears of God Almighty!
It was His hand that brought unto Himself my anxious tears!

O let us never forget despite the seeming triumphs of the foe
That when the world overwhelms us, there is a place we can go
Be it the sin that so easily besets or spiritual wickedness in high places
Under the wings of God Almighty, there is a sure fortress of safety
For when our strength is all used up, and the future is dark and bleak
May we lift our heads to Thine eternal hills; may we fix our eyes on Thee
For there is mercy, there is forgiveness in the sweet countenance of Thy face
There is deliverance! O there *is* deliverance! For Thou hast taught us to pray

November 19, 2016

*(Dedicated to the Prayer Warriors of Emmanuel Temple SDA Church
and to the loving memory of Sis. Olene Lewis)*

For he that toucheth you toucheth the apple of His eye. (Zechariah 2:8, KJV)

Thou That Saveth!

Shew Thy marvelous lovingkindness, O Thou that savest by Thy right hand them which put their trust in Thee from those that rise up against them. Keep me as the apple of the eye, hide me under the shadow of Thy wings. —Psalm 17:7–8 (KJV)

I am in a desert place
Disheartened and dismayed
Separation is what I feared
It is my sin that brought me here
O how I long to see His face
Once more to walk His way
My blinded eyes are searching still
To know Him and be filled
My Lord forgive, restore Thy child
I pray that Thou would reconcile
Thy marvelous lovingkindness show
Thy gift of peace again bestow
For I call upon Thy name
With bended heart in shame
O Thou who saves abundantly
Who saves Thine own unfailingly
And saves utmost and mightily
O Merciful... Save me!

Sometimes we fail the test
We think the enemy rests
Yet steady to our side
Our souls He fiercely tries
Forever on our heels
Intent to bend our will
And wrestles day and night
He fights and fights and fights!
But Thou art God alone
Make haste to save Thine own

Almighty in strength Thou art
Strong Keeper of my heart
Command again this raging sea
That Thou hast always stilled for me
O Thou who saves astoundingly
Who wields Thy power majestically
And saveth still miraculously
Almighty God... Save me!

O Thou who lives to save
From breath unto the grave
Hide us in love between
The sure enfolding of Thy wings
May we with Thee take flight
From all we know of night
And soar the hilltops fair
Bosomed beneath Thy care
If lowlands hold us fast
Our eyes are upward cast
Keep us the apple of Thine eye
When those against us rise
Should we bend to sin's dark call
Upon Thy mercies make us fall
O Thou who saves exceedingly
With eyes that search continually
To show Thy strength victoriously
O Gracious Lord... Save me!

Thy bosom I would dwell
My fears Thy breath shalt quell
And be at peace with Thee
Because Thou loveth me
O save by Thy right hand
Arise that we might stand

Against foes that oppress
And cause our hearts' distress
May to Thy cross we gaze
Upon the One who died to save
The Kindly Prince of Suffering
The Worthy Lamb, the Conquering King
We humbly bow before Thy throne
For who can save, but Thou alone
And thus I ask of Thee
O Thou who saved most graciously
Upon Thy death at Calvary
And arose Thy grave triumphantly
O Redeeming Lord... Save me!

May Thou who saves give ear
To those who hold Thee dear
Upon us breathe not sparingly
But shower most abundantly
Sweet fragrance from above
Fresh dewdrops of Thy love
Assurance we art Thine
Henceforth, yea for all time
Whom Thou giveth rest, has rest
Whom Thou shalt bless, is blest
If we but make request
Thou shall exceed all that we ask
And thus this humble plea
Expressed with love my Lord to Thee
O Thou who saves amazingly
Who saves His child with certainty
And saves for all eternity
O Blessed Savior... Save me!

September 5, 2013

Heal me, O Lord, and I shall be healed; save me, and I shall be saved: for Thou art my praise. (Jeremiah 17:14, KJV)

Unseen

For we wrestle not against flesh and blood, but against principalities,
against powers, against the rulers of the darkness of this world, against
spiritual wickedness in high places. —Ephesians 6:12 (KJV)

Lord, my soul is bent before Thee, bound by pestilence of night
Longing for the joy of morning to dispel these clouds of gloom
The peace that rested in my soul hast fully gone awry
And it seems to me that You have left me too
Upon wearied knees, I feel a vicious battle raging
The winds are rustling fiercely; this storm has come for me
The mighty cohorts of the foe are pressing greatly
And in this festering darkness, Thy face I cannot see

O why hast Thou forsaken me, my Father?
I feel that I've been left out in the cold
Overwhelmed in cares and doubt, I faint, I falter
As I wrestle against this ruthless enemy of my soul
O my heart dost beg that Thou would show Thy tender mercies
For Thy kindnesses hast been my stay throughout these many years
I am now in desperate need of the fullness of Thy presence
While here before Thy Throne of Grace, I fail to see beyond my fears

Though black the threatening skies and blinded are my eyes, Lord
I am casting all my cares on You for Thou hast cared abundantly for me
There are uninvited guests amiss; they are presently before me
But O just a glimpse of Thee would be all this heart would need
Thou hast brought me to this battlefield according to Thy wisdom
For just and perfect are Thy ways, though I am slow of comprehension
And hence on feeble knees I plead, and while I cannot see Thy face
Then by faith alone my soul doth bend in great and hopeful expectation

Another day and this heart again shall know rejoicing
For Thou hast been a Mighty God, a Saving God to me
With still a grateful heart, I worship Thee, I praise Thee
For despite this canopy of dark, I am *seen* beneath Your feet
Whether in the lowest hell or the utmost heights of Heaven
Thou hast ever been my confidant, with mighty arms thereon to lean
For the beauty of Thy gracious love is surely ever-present
And Thy right hand shall uphold me... even if Thou art unseen

Lord, preserve my wretched soul from evil forces of this night
Set Thine angels all around me that I may feel Thy strong embrace
Cover me beneath Thy feathers; may I know that Thou art mine
Till that wondrous, glorious morning, I shall enter into Thy gates
And I shall *gaze* upon Thy beauty—face-to-face!

O mine eyes shall behold Thy Glory—face-to-face!

February 25, 2020

Casting all your care upon Him; for He careth for you. (1 Peter 5:7, KJV)

Love

and

Gratitude

Lord, You know that I love You and am exceedingly grateful for Your lovingkindness and tender mercies. Whenever I reflect upon the scenes of the cross and the ultimate price that was paid for my sins, I continue to be astonished at Your poignant expressions of love. I, too, cry out, as did Your beloved apostle John, as he considered Your incredible gift to this world and exclaimed in sheer amazement and admiration, "Herein is love, not that we loved God, but that He loved us!" (1 John 4:10, KJV). Surely, Father, throughout the endless ages of eternity, we shall marvel still Thy Blessed Calvary and be ever so grateful for the love You have bestowed upon us all!

Canopy of Love

(On the *Carnival Conquest* cruise ship in the Western Caribbean)

I will lift up mine eyes unto the hills, from whence cometh my help. My help cometh from the Lord, which made Heaven and Earth.
—Psalm 121:1–2 (KJV)

In the early dawn hours, we meet here today
beneath Your sweet canopy of love
Your deep blue is rocking a soft lullaby
and Your gentle breeze whispers tenderly Your love
Our communion has never been as sweet as today
as I find on this vessel a most holy place
While beauty surrounds me, bearing gifts from above
I bask in Thy sunshine! I delight in Thy love!

Seems the lessons of the sea are now vivid to me
as a story of old I recall
I see Peter before walking impetuous waves
and turning from Thee, he falls
O may I on life's journey never forget
be it storms, boisterous winds, billowing waves
that I to the hills will ever lift up mine eyes
from whence doth cometh my aid
For my help cometh from Thee, O Lord
whom this haven of rest Thou hast formed
How awesome Thy power! How great is Thy strength!
How mighty to save is Thine arm!

Remind me continually that our footsteps are sure
when ordered and fashioned by Thee
That no forces of evil can conquer the soul
whose eyes remain fixed upon Thee
The cruel world may hate us; our friends may desert us
yet upon Thy dear bosom we'll stay

When the pain overwhelms us, Thy presence sustains us
and how sweetly Thou comfort our days

As the sun sets with rare beauty, I, too, bow at Your feet
beneath Your sweet canopy of love
Your deep blue is rocking a soft lullaby
as You embrace me with whispers of love!

March 8, 2004

(Dedicated to Vivian & William Crawford)

Charmed in Beauty

The entrance of Thy words giveth light; it giveth understanding unto the simple. —Psalm 119:130 (KJV)

Charmed in beauty is His voice
That takes my breath away
My heart delights in all His words
As He transforms night to day
Great treasures worth a thousand fold
To those who would believe
What other pleasure can compare
To sitting at His feet

His words are breath and life to me
I would know no other way
But pray that He would guard my steps
That I may never stray
And O to be thus led by God
Is to have His peace divine
Unfolding blessings ever near
That are absolutely mine!

Charmed in beauty are His words
His voice clothed in righteousness
He speaks and how He warms the hearts
Of all who would be blest
I greatly linger at His feet
And embrace His words to me
No other sound to grace my life
Is as sweet and comforting

If only those who know Thee not
Would simply "taste and see"
They would marvel at Thy gracious love
Their lives would be made free

Their hearts would stand in wondrous awe
As they are raised to glorious heights
For Thy words give understanding
Its very entrance gives us light

O Lord, may we be ever drawn
To the beauty of Thy Word
Prepare our minds to understand
The truths that we have heard
Thus we can be the lesser lights
That lead lost souls to Thee
For Thou alone can pierce men's hearts
And set the captives free

Yes clothed in beauty is Thy voice
That greets me when I wake
And beautiful Thy whisperings
Before my slumber takes
Until that day I see Thy face
And bow down to my King
May I love Thy law, may I bless Thy name
May my voice Thy praises sing!

May 25, 2012

My heart standeth in awe of Thy word. (Psalm 119:161, KJV)

Crucify!

But they cried, saying, "Crucify Him, crucify Him."
—Luke 23:21 (KJV)

We have brought Him here today
Bound in chains, no words to say
Yet within our hearts to each of us He speaks
As we gaze upon His form
Where's the hope we should have borne
In the knowledge that He died for you and me

For it was there upon a cross
That our Savior suffered loss
And today we pierce His wounded side again
I can almost hear the cry
From the spotless Lamb on high
As we pound the nails into His loving hands

I can hear the jeering crowd
Reviling voices, cruel and loud
"Crucify Him! Crucify Him! Crucify!"
Shall we take His life today
By the things we do and say
For we do no less when Him our hearts deny

I still hear the prayer He said
As He bends His thorn-pierced head
"Father forgive; for they know not what they do"
Even ere death He sought to save
Facing Himself a darkly grave
While pleading mercy upon the ignorant and the cruel

So let us join this maddening throng
Spit upon the Christ we've wronged
Declare our rage upon the dying Prince of Peace

We'll then wash our blood-stained hands
Of this Christ, the Son of Man
Who gave His all in perfect love for you and me

Yes, I brought Him here today
Bound in chains, no words to say
Crowned with sharply thorns to mock His Royal Majesty
And as I gaze upon the Christ
I still cry, "Crucify!"
As this same Jesus dies again with an astounding love for me!

November 15, 1988

Then said Jesus, "Father, forgive them; for they know not what they do." (Luke 23:34, KJV)

He Calls My Name

But Mary stood outside by the tomb weeping, and as she wept she stooped down and looked into the tomb. And she saw two angels in white sitting, one at the head and the other at the feet, where the body of Jesus had lain. Then they said to her, "Woman, why are you weeping?" She said to them, "Because they have taken away my Lord, and I do not know where they have laid Him." Now when she had said this, she turned around and saw Jesus standing there, and did not know that it was Jesus. Jesus said to her, "Woman, why are you weeping? Whom are you seeking?" She, supposing Him to be the gardener, said to Him, "Sir, if You have carried Him away, tell me where You have laid Him, and I will take Him away." Jesus said to her, "Mary!" She turned and said to Him, "Rabboni!" —John 20:11–16 (NKJV)

He calls my name
And my soul is hushed by His presence
My heart is awed and filled
As I bow before the Master's will
And I marvel that He calls to me
And am humbled by His company
For His voice is all that is comforting
When Jesus calls my name

"Why weepest thou?"
Such caring words my Lord still speaks
For He would turn my tears to gladness
And vanish every trace of sadness
No need to fear the dark
For His presence lights the heart
And His words—O how they charm
The Word made flesh in loving arms
To shelter me from this world's harm
Indeed, "this is the Christ"
My Beloved Rabboni

"Whom seekest thou?"
O, but the Omniscient already knows
For He would have it so that I
Would never leave His pierced side
Yet with blinding tears of grief I say
"They have carried my Precious Lord away
And I do not know where He's been laid
He is the One I seek"

And then... Heaven's Majesty speaks
"Mary!"
I turn and fully recognize
The Savior there before my eyes
O what joy! This cannot be!
The Risen Christ of Calvary
To think that I would utter cries
When Thou wast right here by my side
My heart is full; with joy I'm raised
From cursed to blessed, from grief to praise
Yes, the precious Lamb of Calvary
With compassionate love addresses me
And I fall prostrate at His feet
Ever grateful He hast set me free

And still today He calls His child
Whose sight is dimmed by darkened clouds
And raises her from sin's dark grave
With nail-scarred hands stretched forth to save
He calls, and His children know His voice
And thus they ever shall rejoice
For when the Master calls your name
Your life is never quite the same

Henceforth, I'll praise His name
For the scars of redeeming love He bears
For catching the fall of my every tear
For silencing storms with His presence
And honoring me with full acceptance

I am yet amazed that He calls for me
And I am humbled by His company
For His voice is O so comforting
When Jesus calls my name

July 19, 2013

(To my granddaughter, Brittany)

*My sheep hear My voice, and I know them, and
they follow Me. (John 10:27, KJV)*

"Herein is Love"

*I have heard of Thee by the hearing of the ear: but now
mine eye seeth Thee. —Job 42:5 (KJV)*

*Herein is love, not that we loved God, but that
He loved us. —1 John 4:10 (KJV)*

I have heard of His virgin birth
And how marveled and amazed were the heavens and Earth
When at last, the Deliverer of Israel had come
The Heavenly Father sent forth His son
And now unto us a Savior is born
The treasure of earth, though lowly adorned
The Promised Messiah, who had long been foretold
Lies sweet in a manger, more precious than gold
The heavens are hushed, and the angels are bowed
Stooping to gaze upon the princely child
And joins in chorus to the Heavenly Sent
*"Glory to God in the highest
and on Earth peace, good will toward men."*

Many stories I have heard of His life
His miraculous healing of the lame and the blind
A minister to those who are burdened in sin
Forgiving and uplifting the souls of men
Divinity soothing the woes of humanity
Delivering from hell and all its depravity
And no one He turns away
For He hast come that all may be saved
Yes, surely He is full of mercy and grace
And though I had not seen Him face to face
A flicker of hope from within me is stirred
As I ponder and question all that I've heard

They tell too of His death at the cross
How He sacrificed all in spite of great loss
And though the full scope, I cannot conceive
I was told that He died, even for me
Thus to Calvary I hastened and anxiously stood
Till I felt the pure warmth of His covering blood
Astonished and humbled at The Lamb's sacrifice
I fall prostrate, realizing His death gives me life
And exclaim: O indeed, "Herein is love!
Not that we loved God, but that He loved us"
I was blind, but with wonder, now I can see!
And pray His cleansing blood would purify me
Wash not only my feet, Lord, but my hands and my head
It is because the Redeemer hast died in my stead
That I may approach "Him that sitteth on the Throne"
Claiming the gift for which His Son has atoned

By the hearing of the ear, I have heard of Thee
But now with mine own eyes, I am beholding Thee
That I may ever gaze upon the beauty of Thy face
For I know now Thy mercies; I have tasted Thy grace
The words Thou dost speak, I hold absolute dear
They have given me great peace; they have vanished my fears
I've been rescued! I've been pardoned! I have been set free!
It is enough! It *is* enough that His blood covers me!

O today, won't you behold the Lamb...
The Most Sweet Beloved of Calvary
The High and Lifted Up upon that ole rugged cross
Jesus Christ who gave His life for you and me

O today, behold the Triumphant King
With your own eyes, lift up your heads and see

See Him clothed in righteousness, enshrouded in pure light
Worthy of the highest praise, dominion, power and might
For in Him resides all knowledge, wisdom, holiness and strength
Blessings and honor and glory and majesty all belongs to Him
Yes, marvel thou, O heavens! and be truly amazed, O earth!
As our eyes behold the Christ for whom ours ears hath thusly heard
And from everlasting to everlasting, as we behold the One Beloved
O we shall be made astonished still... for saints, "Herein is love!"
We shall be made *astonished*, for this, indeed, is love!

February 27, 2019

Glory to God in the highest, and on Earth peace,
good will toward men. (Luke 2:14, KJV)

I Marvel at Calvary!

And when they were come to the place, which is called Calvary, there they crucified Him. —Luke 23:33 (KJV)

As I reflect upon Your gracious love
I am exceedingly amazed
That when a prayer escapes my sinful lips
It is held beneath Your gaze
As Your ear inclines from Heaven
Not a word is lost, unheard
But is caught up with haste unto Thyself
Such regard is undeserved

What is man for whom Your tenderest thoughts
Are expressed in passionate tones
Resonating to this woeful earth
From the aura of Thine own Throne
O I marvel, Lord, at such stunning love
Though I fail to comprehend just how
Thou, the Adored of Heaven
Could come to love one such as I

And thus, I marvel, Lord, at Calvary
As Thy cross is lifted before mine eyes
Thy bleeding nail-pierced hands and feet
Thy thorn-pierced brow and wounded side
I am beholden to Thy precious blood
That Thou in love didst shed for me
And fall awestruck before the Lamb of God
For if not for the cross, Lord, where would I be?

And they ask me why I love Thee
O the tears at once began to flow
Beneath a bended brow that would ne'er forget
How from the pit of hell Thou delivered my soul

I am unworthy, Lord, yet Thou gave Thine everything
And I have nothing, nothing! What can I offer Thee?
But a most sinful, broken and contrite heart
That, too, wast pierced... at Calvary

These uncleaned lips are at an utter loss
To speak of a love so profoundly great
That would leave the splendor of Thine Heavenly Throne
To die for those who would spurn Thy grace
Thy poignant eyes at Calvary's cross
Hast met my own, unmasked, ashamed
And now my wanting heart seeks Thine
That I may live to bless Thy name

O I marvel, Lord, at Calvary
Thy cross is ever before mine eyes
Thy bleeding nail-pierced hands and feet
Thy thorn-pierced brow and wounded side
I am beholden to Thy precious blood
That Thou in love didst spill for me
And fall stricken before the Lamb of God
In everlasting awe of Calvary

Even now—and still with wide-eyed wonder
As I view His form upon that tree—
I am amazed! I am yet astounded
For what the Son of God hast done for me!
And very soon His eyes shall meet mine own
As He lifts me up unto eternity
I will bless the Lamb, O my soul!
I will bless the Lamb, O my soul!
I will bless the Lamb, O my soul...
For what His blood hast done for me
O Thou, Sweet Beloved of Calvary

Throughout the endless ages of eternity
Ah, we shall marvel still His Holy Majesty!
We shall marvel still His life, His death at Calvary
We shall marvel still His Risen Christ, The King of Kings!
And shall proclaim His Worthy Name...
From everlasting to everlasting!

We shall bless and exalt Thy name, O Thou My Christ...
For everlasting!

April 20, 2018

*But He was wounded for our transgressions, He was bruised
for our iniquities: the chastisement of our peace was upon Him;
and with His stripes we are healed. (Isaiah 53:5, KJV)*

Make My Heart to Love Thee!

And thou shalt love the Lord thy God with all thine heart, and with all thy soul, and with all thy might. —Deuteronomy 6:5 (KJV)

Thy love for me is great, O Lord
and I am indeed most grateful
Thou art my song in the discord of life
my warm covering from the frigid cold of night
Thou hast taken my pain
formed and shaped it by fire
into altars—
yes, altars of praise, from out of misery, raised
and of Heaven, empowered
all to bless Thee, O Lord, to exalt and to honor Thy name
applauding Thy faithfulness
over and over again

I am awed by Thy stunning beauty and grace
I am amazed by Thy power and unsearchable ways
I delight in Thy love for Thou art wondrously fair
and when considering the depths of Thine infinite care
I am unable to guard or to silence my tears...
for it is utterly incomprehensible
that Thou, who art exceedingly merciful and gracious
views me in Thy sight as most precious
and although I am poor and unlovely
altogether sinful and unworthy
Thy life, even so, Thou willingly gave
for my wretched soul to save

As such, I implore Thee, O Lord...
make my heart to adore Thee
with a perfect and beautiful love—
the same Thou hast showered on me
enduring, endearing, everlasting

And if *my* love can never measure to Thine
and is found wanting and far beneath the Divine
still Lord... may it ever be abundantly sweet
and devoted for always and *only* to Thee
for the yearning of my heart is to love Thee, O Lord
with the great love Thou hath lavished on me

O make my heart to love Thee, Lord...
exceedingly, exceptionally, eternally!

March 10, 2021

Tears of Jesus

Jesus wept. —John 11:35 (KJV)

The tears of Jesus
From a sorrowful heart
Tender and pitying
Most precious they are
Beneath the cross they fall
Embracing every race
Compassionate, Saving Lord
Tears marked His face

He weeps with those who weep
But His tears mean more
Than shattered dreams and lives
His heart is sore
Must He forever call
In pleading tones
His wandering prodigals
He craves His own

Must Thou, Lord, weep for me
Thy blessed face stained
With marks of bitter teardrops
For all that I am
"O Jerusalem!" Thou cried
Could that city be me
If only I knew
The things which belong to my peace

And near Lazarus' grave
If only they could see
That the tears You shed
Was for them... and me

Your groaning, piercing pain
Over our distress and fears
A heart that loves mankind
Is what brought those tears

Blessed tears of God
Mourning for our sins
Forever He shall weep
Until we're safe in Him
Sacred tears of Jesus
Can we understand
The love our Lord bestows
Upon sinful man

March 26, 1980

Saying, "If thou hadst known, even thou, at least in this thy day the things which belong unto thy peace! but now they are hid from thine eyes." (Luke 19:42, KJV)

Thou Art Gracious!

And it shall come to pass, when he crieth unto Me, that I will hear; for I am gracious. —Exodus 22:27 (KJV)

Thou art most Gracious, Lord
Merciful, Compassionate
The full of Thine attributes
Cannot be uttered or expressed
For there is no other hand, but Thine
That surpasses all in strength and might
And navigates the very depths of hell
That I may ascend to glorious heights

What other worthy sway can be
That woos my weary, wandering soul
Flying swiftly to my fallen path
Overshadowing me, before I ask
Beyond my dreadful faults, Thou sees
And would my captive soul reclaim
Still, Lord, Thou surely loveth me
And holds dear my lowly frame

Thou art most Gracious, Lord
And I come hesitant, ashamed
Unmasked, unkept and pitiful
Unworthy to speak Thine holy name
Yet, Thou with tenderness of heart
Doth from Thine habitation bend
With lovingkindness in Thine eyes
To rescue still and calls me "friend"

Though I would firmly shut mine eyes
As if to hide myself from Thee
Yet through the guilt, the hurt, the shame
Thy face is all mine eyes can see
For Thou remains still Gracious, Lord
Though I am fallen, tempted, tried
And keeps Thy promise ne'er to leave
Those who cleave onto Thy side

And when the battle knows no end
And I grow weary of sleepless nights
And faint beneath the enemy's hand
All torn and worn, no power or might
Beneath Thy wings, Thou cradles me
As to Thy bosom I retreat
I find Thou standing in my stead
Fighting my battles vicariously

Thus at Thy nail-scarred feet I fall
Unfit to approach Thy Father's Throne
Thou covers me with Thine own robe
That all Heaven knows to whom I belong
What awesome love! What tenderest care!
What unsurpassed generosity!
That He who sits upon the Throne
Hast availed Himself to one such as me

And when the end of time has come
And I no more am tossed about
But in Thine arms, I shall ever be
The grateful child of the Lord Most High
O everlasting shall be my love to Thee!
Yes, everlasting shall be my praises!

For when my lips cried out to Thee
Thou answered, forthwith and mightily
Even though there is nothing that is good in me
Thou answered... for Thou art Gracious!

March 25, 2019

(Dedicated to Joanie Hamilton with thanks!)

Gracious is the Lord, and righteous; yea, our God is merciful. (Psalm 116:5, KJV)

For if ye turn again unto the Lord, your brethren and your children shall find compassion before them that lead them captive, so that they shall come again into this land: for the Lord your God is gracious and merciful, and will not turn away His face from you, if ye return unto Him. (2 Chronicles 30:9, KJV)

"What Manner of Love!"

*Behold, what manner of love the Father hath bestowed upon us, that
we should be called the sons of God: therefore the world knoweth us
not, because it knew Him not. —1 John 3:1 (KJV)*

Sometimes in moments of quiet
When alone I sit at His feet
And sweetly commune with the Father
My heart from within me leaps
For how can I, the chiefest of sinners
Partake of His riches above
With joy, I cry out in amazement
"Behold, what manner of love!"

"Behold, what manner of love
The Father has bestowed upon us"
To be called the sons and daughters of God
And heirs of the heavenly trust
What privilege it is to behold Him
Full of mercy, compassion and grace
Having the blessed assurance that hereafter
We shall then see Him face to face

O what joy! I can barely contain it!
O what joy that is abundantly mine!
The One *Altogether Lovely* in Heaven
Is altogether faithful and kind
We have been purchased with blood by our Savior
A greater sacrifice could not have been made
O the debt that I owe to this Lover of Souls
Who paid the price for my soul to save

So with awe let us come in His chambers
And let His Sweet Spirit abide

Ever mindful the Father in Heaven
Is the same Father who is here by our sides
Let us humbly acknowledge His presence
As do the heavenly courts up above
For we are the sons and daughters of the Almighty God
O "behold, what manner of love!"

February 24, 2012

(To my grandson-in-law, Steve)

"Will a Man Rob God?"

Will a man rob God? —Malachi 3:8 (KJV)

Have you ever knelt to pray
But didn't know just what to say
You feel unworthy to approach His throne
So greatly burdened and alone
You doubt your prayers can even rise
Beyond this darkness to heavenly skies
Yet somehow through the guilt and shame
You remember God's Gift and with joy exclaim
"Praise to the Lamb of Calvary!
His bloodstained robe now covers me
So when I fall on bended knee
It is His Son the Father sees"
My heart grows full just from that thought
How is it then that I *rob* my God?

Have you ever left the Master's care
And stumbled into the devil's snare
This enemy will take you down
Make no mistake to where you're bound
He will take you places far and low
To where you thought you'd never go
He leaves you helpless and alone
Until it seems all hope is gone
Your heart grows faint with dread and fear
There is no comfort, only tears
But then you remember your Father's place
And you long to see His loving face
In your distress, His name you call
And into His outstretched arms you fall

He holds you close and welcomes you
Like no other friend could ever do
He never leaves us, nor forsakes
And He forgives our tired and sad mistakes
He fills our hearts with joy and peace
So that once again, we are free
O how wonderful and sweet the thought
How is it then that we *rob* our God?

Such blessings that the Father gives
A shelter strong wherein we live
A peace that man can't understand
A forgiving God, a faithful friend
A mighty Conqueror indeed
Who contends with those that contend with me
He is fierce in battle, strong and true
And He does what no other defender can do
A Comforter, a Prince, a King
Who reigns with healing in His wings
He is our daily confidant
Our source of joy, our trust, our strength
He fills our hearts with songs to sing
He is to us our everything!
How marvelous what love He's wrought!
How is it then that we *rob* our God?

"Prove Me now herewith" the Father pleas
"And the windows of Heaven I will open to thee"
His bountiful goodness He will freely outpour
As He blesses and blesses and blesses us more
How gracious, how precious, how amazing His love!
How disturbing the question: "Will a man rob God?"

April 22, 2011

Will a man rob God? Yet ye have robbed Me.
But ye say, Wherein have we robbed Thee? In tithes and offerings.
Ye are cursed with a curse: for ye have robbed Me, even this whole nation.
Bring ye all the tithes into the storehouse, that there may be meat in
Mine house, and prove Me now herewith, saith the Lord of Hosts,
if I will not open you the windows of Heaven, and pour you out a
blessing, that there shall not be room enough to receive it.
And I will rebuke the devourer for your sakes, and he
shall not destroy the fruits of your ground;
neither shall your vine cast her fruit before the
time in the field, saith the Lord of Hosts.
And all nations shall call you blessed:
for ye shall be a delightsome land, saith the
Lord of Hosts. (Malachi 3:8–12, KJV)

And blessed be the Most High God, which hath delivered thine enemies into thy hand. And he gave Him tithes of all. (Genesis 14:20, KJV)

You and Me

For He hath said, I will never leave thee, nor forsake thee.
—Hebrews 13:5 (KJV)

Thou calls me from my slumber, and I feel Thy presence sweet
My soul is hushed with wonder, and I am awed by Thy mystique
I can almost trace the outline of Thy kind and loving face
And I smile for no one knows
that Thou hast journeyed through time and space
and doth visit me in the quiet of this midnight hour
As I feel Thy breath upon me
I yield solely to its power
and would beg, Lord, that Thou never leave
never make this heart to grieve
Let it be like this for always...
You and me

The writings penned beneath my hands are sweet because of Thee
for Thou hast filled my lips with praise, gratitude, rejoicing
My heart is overwhelmed that Thou wouldst come down from above
and surround me with Thy glory
bathing me richly in Thy love
O before my eyes are closed in sleep, I pray when I awake
Thou will still be near beside me
Never leave, nor forsake
Thou hast promised me, my Lord
and with whole heart, I would believe
it will be like this for always...
You and me

And when at last in our heavenly home where we will part no more
I shall ever be through eternity with whom my heart adores

O my eyes shall behold Thy beauty
as with the redeemed I too shall sing
of Thy great and tenderest mercies wrought in love
at Calvary

But in the stillness of this hour where a wanting heart is made Thy throne
as it pleases Thee, my Beloved King, hold me close and keep me as Thine own
And on the morrow when the foe makes haste to overthrow Thy reign
be Thou swift and fierce in battle ere I call upon Thy name
O make it so, my Gracious Lord, make it so and it shall be
that my heart would know no other
that my eyes seek only Thee
that my soul would breathe Thy spirit
and to those whose steps I meet
may I share the full and abundant life
that only comes from knowing Thee

As this sacred hour draws to its close, may I hold onto its memory
and, too, the God who loves me so, may He ne'er depart from me
He didst make my slumbering soul awake
and covered me with His embrace
made my wingless soul to fly
and I am satisfied
As I muse upon His gracious heart
I am humbled by His kind regard
For in the night, my Most Sweet Beloved
condescends that I may know His love
And I beg that He would never leave
never take this joy away from me
O make it so, my Gracious Lord
Make it so and let it be
just like this for always...
You and me

And lo!
I hear the voice of My Most Beloved
whisper soft and assuringly:

"O it *is* so! My doubting child
I have spoken! And it *is* so!
I promised I would never leave
and hereafter, ye shall know
Though sure the fullness of this hour
(O thou have yet to know true bliss)
henceforth, My child, and forevermore
it will be indeed *much* more than this!

For ye shall be with Me for always
Yes, for always—
you and Me"

April 2, 2018

Thine eyes shall see the King in His beauty. (Isaiah 33:17, KJV)

Praise

and

Thanksgiving

ABUNDANT PRAISE • HE CAME FOR ME • HIS DELIGHT • HIS LOVELY AND HIS GREAT!
I WILL ALWAYS HAVE A SONG • LIFTER OF MY HEART • MY HEART IS FULL
NEVER FORGET • NONE LIKE THEE • SACRIFICE OF PRAISE!
THE OBJECT OF MY PRAISE • WHAT SHALL I RENDER

There is something about praising God that elevates us to a higher level, that transports us to the sweet and beautiful aura of heavenly places. When experiencing difficulties in our lives, if we would recall God's gratuitous blessings in our past and lift our heads to the heavens and utter the beloved testimonies of His exceptional and manifold goodness, God will inhabit our praises, for He delights in the gratitude and adoration of His children. And where God resides, there is peace and comfort! Where God resides, there is celebration and rejoicing! There is abundant praise and unceasing thanksgiving in the glorious presence of our Father! "Oh that men would praise the Lord for His goodness, and for His wonderful works to the children of men!" (Psalm 107:31, KJV)

Abundant Praise!

But now thus saith the Lord that created thee, O Jacob, and He that formed thee, O Israel, Fear not: for I have redeemed thee, I have called thee by thy name; thou art Mine. —Isaiah 43:1 (KJV)

O Thou, who creates by the power of Thine hand
I bear witness Thou, too, art an ever-present friend
I confess to Thy goodness that hast followed my days
And respond to Thy grace with an abundance of praise

Of my pain and my grief, Thine own heart sympathized
Sending the Angel of Thy Presence to redeem me in trials
Not a sigh, nor a tear, but reverberates with Thy love
And with tender, pitying mercy Thy dost bend from above

O Thy deliverance hast been mighty in the pestilence of night
When I called, Thou hast answered, "My child, here am I"
With trembling lips I adore Thee for Thou hast rescued my soul
And hast made me to follow Thee wheresoever Thou go

How can it be that one such as lowly as I
Could freely bask in the warmth that Thy presence provides
And be privileged to gaze upon the beauty of Thy face
And to know Thy kind mercies and tenderest embrace

Who would think that mere man with his troubles and woes
Can ascend to the heavens gathering treasures untold
And to hear as one sits at His Majesty's feet
"Thou art Mine!" O words of comfort, so incredibly sweet!

I *am* His! And upon my lips there are no other words
I am *His*! A child of Glory, henceforth and forevermore

And even now, lips quivering still, as I behold Thy kind face
Thou *too* art mine! For always Lord, my Sweet Abundance of Praise!
Thou too art mine! O Blest Redeemer, I am *full* with Thy praise!
Yes Thou art mine! O Darling of Heaven! I shall ever honor Thee with praise!

July 25, 2015

(Dedicated to Arlene Husband)

I am my Beloved's, and my Beloved is mine. (Song of Solomon 6:3, KJV)

He Came for Me

Where wast thou when I laid the foundations of the earth?
—Job 38:4 (KJV)

He came for me—the enemy
O he is an insidious foe
splattering heavy, darkly blotches
against skies once blue
casting elongated shadows
in painful, sickly, deathly hues
sowing toxins that destroy the mind
in a land I do not recognize
with thousands falling at my side
and none to console the fears and cries
He intoxicates, manipulates
vying ruthless for my soul
as I walk in terror of the night
dodging arrows in the broad daylight
thus in agony, I am doomed to live
and alone, I am doomed to die

And how the darkness deepens—
though subtly, yet steadily
for this foe is keen and shrewd
and will not stop till he consumes
O it seems, Lord, I cannot endure
Thou hast made my steps slow and unsure
Thou hast plagued my soul with suffering
beneath kings with unsound reasoning
Where is the strength of Thy right hand
that makes the staggering child to stand?
Art Thou not acquainted with all my days?
Doth Thou not guard and perfect my ways?
O this is an easy thing for Thee
to deliver from the hand of the enemy

but instead, I am hurled into blackest night
devoid of joy and peace of mind
and beg unto Thee, "O plead my cause!
Arise! Save me!... with Everlasting arms!"

And then...
He came for me—The Savior
with sweet reiterations of *His* power
for He, the renowned Creator
doth pierce the blackness of this hour
I hear Him as He plainly speaks
chastising me with questionings:
"'Where was *thou* when I laid the foundations of the Earth'
or hung the moon in the heavens; didst *thou* observe?
Doth *thou* hold authority over the sea and its waves
commanding the waters, and they forthwith obey?
'Canst thou bind the sweet influences of Pleiades'
or loosen Orion's bands?
Doth thou have the knowledge and power and might
to uphold constellations in thy hands?
'Doth the hawk fly by *thy* wisdom'
as she stretches her wings to the south?
'Doth the eagle mount up at *thy* command'
making her nest on high?
'Hast thou an arm like God?
Canst thou thunder with a voice like Him?'
Presumeth thou to instruct the Almighty
and reprove Him with whom thy soul contends?"

O no Lord; I cannot hold in check
Thy hundred billion stars
or have knowledge of Thy Universe
and the vast constellations thereof

for woe is me; I am nothing!
I am simple, wretched and vile
unworthy indeed to give answer to He
who embodies all wisdom, all power and might
Thou binds the star cluster of Pleiades
Thou alone can loosen Orion's belt
Thy dominion is over the land and the seas
commanding the wind, hail and thunders of light
Thine ears are open unto the heavens
but still Thou art tuned to *my* cries
and in spite of the enormity of my sins
in spite of the strength of the enemy's hand
Thou doth penetrate still the defiant black skies
to mightily rescue Thy child

O Thou hast heard my cries from Heaven
afar from Celestial Courts, I was seen
and was humbled at the utterances of Thy greatness
and made strong by Thy power to redeem
O I am enthralled that His Beloved Majesty
enshrouded in power and unsurpassed excellency
arose, great and almighty, from His illustrious throne
wielding such love—yet to be seen or known
and condescends to this woeful earth
in swaddling garbs of a lowly birth
that *He* might answer the urgent plea…
"Save *me*!"

He came for me!

But… if by The Omnipotent hand I am slain
I will look to the heavens; my trust shall remain
for my Redeemer one day in the clouds shall appear
at the sound of the trumpet—O His coming is near

and He shall wipe away sorrow, dry every tear
erase every cumbersome fear
Yes, Jesus, for me, is coming again
and I—O what joy!—shall forever be with Him!

Jesus is coming for me!

December 31, 2020

Though He slay me, yet will I trust in Him. (Job 13:15, KJV)

Where wast thou when I laid the foundations of the earth?
declare, if thou hast understanding. (Job 38:4, KJV)

Canst thou bind the sweet influences of Pleiades or
loose the bands of Orion? (Job 38:31, KJV)

Doth the hawk fly by thy wisdom, and stretch her wings toward
the south? Doth the eagle mount up at thy command,
and make her nest on high? (Job 39:26–27, KJV)

Hast thou an arm like God? or canst thou thunder
with a voice like Him? (Job 40:9, KJV)

Shall he that contendeth with the Almighty instruct Him?
he that reproveth God, let him answer it. (Job 40:2, KJV)

His Delight

Woe to them that go down to Egypt for help; and stay on horses, and trust in chariots, because they are many; and in horsemen, because they are very strong; but they look not unto the Holy One of Israel, neither seek the Lord! —Isaiah 31:1 (KJV)

The Lord our God is a dwelling place
He is a stronghold in this world of endless cares
In His arms there is gladness unsurpassing
And His own strength where we would find despair
He is our Peace when all around us hearts are failing
In utter darkness, He is the Eternal Prince of Light
His matchless love is forever etched upon the inwards of our hearts
To be shared... for this is His delight!

His kingdom is from everlasting to everlasting
Spirit and power are the treasured words He speaks
Glory and Majesty enshrouds His Hallowed Presence
He, the Strength of Israel, never slumbers, never sleeps
And if *this* be our God, then the victory *now* is ours
For yet today, all our battles He will fight
And darkness trembles and crumbles when He rolls His voice as thunder
O to rescue... this is His delight!

There are some who put their trust in chariots
In mighty warriors with horses, shields and swords
Not knowing that success is not about numbers or strength
But battles are won in the name of the Lord
We are, therefore, "more than conquerors"
What! Shall we then fear the enemy's might?
When the sound of every battle cry echoes *first* from His Throne on high
To give God the glory... for this is His delight!

O the earth is still full of His goodness
From age to age, His lovingkindness has never changed
The great storehouse of His riches are ever flowing
And it is ours, if we would but ask in His name
He is a shelter for all who are wearied
A mighty fortress, a refuge, a friend
The Beloved, who is all merciful, full of compassion, gracious and bountiful
Forever bending to uplift the souls of men

If you should find *yourself* in a desert place
With a heart scorched and burned by unquenchable flames
Then I invite you to drink of the wellsprings of Jesus
You can now hear the sound of an abundance of rain
"Get thee up, eat and drink," for the journey is great
We must meet this dark foe in the deep of the night
But this we do know with the utmost assurance
Jesus Saves... from the depths of hell to Heaven's endless heights
Jesus Saves... from the stench of death to the sweet savor of new life
Jesus Saves... in wondrous splendor and with excellency of pure power and all might!

Jesus Saves! Now and forever! O *this* is truly His delight!

June 3, 2016

(Dedicated to the Slocumb Family)

*Some trust in chariots, and some in horses: but we will remember
the name of the Lord our God. (Psalm 20:7, KJV)*

*Get thee up, eat and drink; for there is a sound
of abundance of rain. (1 Kings 18:41, KJV)*

*Nay, in all these things we are more than conquerors
through Him that loved us. (Romans 8:37, KJV)*

His Lovely and His Great!

For how great is God's goodness and how great is His beauty!
—Zechariah 9:17 (AMP)

He kisses tenderly my brow and makes my slumber sweet
And cradles me most lovingly in the midst of the angry deep
The maddening roar of waves and seas—it is but a lullaby
As my Sweet Beloved stands guard against the terrors of the night

A shelter in the time of storm, a delight when skies are fair
In deep of sleep or in wake of day, I am safe beneath His care
And who is he that would disturb a child of Heaven's grace
Who hast made her trust beneath the wings of the Lovely and the Great

The Lovely... as He is wondrously fair! O His beauty is untold!
The Fairest of Ten Thousands who hast stooped to save my soul
The Great... for He is mighty and holds all power in His hands
And hast fought the vicious tempter just to redeem the hearts of men

And who is this stately Prince in whom perfection of beauty resides
Enshroud in majesty and grace, I say, this *is* the Christ!
For with His strength and beauty He hast claimed my grateful heart
That I may know Him as He is and share all He would impart

O how my stammering tongue falls short and fails at words to say
To tell how He hast rescued me and hast brought me from the grave
For truly His goodness and mercy hast followed me all of my days
O Thou, Sweet Blessed of Israel, it is Thy Lovely that hast made Thee Great

And how my soul dost ache and yearn for that most-awaited day
When the clouds shall part as the heavens declare His coming in grand array
O His eyes shall meet mine eyes, and His smile shall greet my face
And I shall give praise abundantly, unashamed and O most lavishly
With all that is inside of me...
Unto His Lovely and His Great

Yes, I shall give praise exceedingly, unreserved and truly gratefully
For all that He hast done for me...
Unto His Lovely and His Great

Indeed, I shall give praise unceasingly, tearful but O so joyfully
Throughout the full expanse of eternity...
Unto His Lovely and His Great!

Unto Thee, my Most Beloved, Thou art Lovely! Thou art Great!
O it is Thy *love* that hast made Thee Beautiful!
It is Thy *love* that hast made Thee Great!

January 1, 2016

(To my daughter, Aurora)

Yea, He is altogether lovely. (Song of Solomon 5:16, KJV)

For great is the Lord, and greatly to be praised. (1 Chronicles 16:25, KJV)

I Will Always Have a Song

Yet the Lord will command His lovingkindness in the daytime, and in the
night His song shall be with me, and my prayer unto the God of my life.
—Psalm 42:8 (KJV)

The road of life has many turns along the way
There are depths to which one falls where there is no light of day
For the enemy is determined to lead our feet astray
Still… out of the pitfalls of life
Though constant and unyielding it seems the fight
Out of the winds, the rains and the floods
God is still working it out for our good
And He who is faithful will honor our trust
And hast promised to finish what He started in us
There is nothing to fear
For as long as He's near
He will gladden our hearts with a song

And thus, I will always have a song
For He hast made me to know to whom I belong
Though I have questioned the clouds that hast darkened my skies
And can't find the answers to the hows and the whys
And the burdens be heavy and friends leave my side
And I feel that my spirit will shrivel up and die
But O for the mercies He's shown
And His faithfulness to each of His own
He blesses me still
With His strength I am filled
As He refreshes my life with a song

O yes, I will always have a song
A praise of deliverance O Lord unto Thee
For Thou who art clothed in untouchable light
Hast reflected Thy beams in the darkest of night

My Savior, my Deliverer, the Love of My Life
The Hidden Treasure of Heaven, the Pearl of Great Price
The Altogether Lovely, the Lamb Forever Worthy
Sweet Bosom of Rest in whom all nations are blest
Thou hast conquered my fears and hast kissed away my tears
And hast swallowed up my enemies in the parting of Thy mighty seas
Thou, O Wonderful Savior, Sweet Gifter of Psalms to me
Thou hast given me sight in the blackest of night
And I give all honor and glory to Thee!

O yes, I will always have a song
A never-ending love song my heart shall forever sing
An everlasting coronation of indebted love and adoration
Upon His Majesty, the Almighty King of Kings!

March 31, 2014

(Dedicated to Sis. Barbara Crawford)

Lifter of My Heart

But Thou, O Lord, art a shield for me; my glory, and the lifter up of mine head.
—Psalm 3:3 (KJV)

O Thou, the Lifter of my head
Who draws my praise in deep of night
And raises me even unto Thee
And clothes me with Thy robe of light
What wondrous joy it is to be
The daughter of the Most High King
My heart is all consumed by Thee
For Thou hast given life to me

What priceless treasures Thou hast poured
Upon this lowly soul of mine
Unworthy, yet Thy choicest gifts
Are showered full with love divine
My heart cries out in gratefulness
My lips proclaim Thy excellence
If only all would taste and see
They would bow before Thy Majesty

O Gracious Lifter of my thoughts
I ponder still what Thou hast wrought
How can it be that Thou wouldst give
Thy love in blood that I might live
I marvel at this gift bestowed
Such love! It causes tears to flow
And makes my soul Thine heart to seek
For I am naught apart from Thee

And how Thy tenderness makes known
That Thou art gracious to Thine own
Thine heart of love that searches low
That I might in Thy graces grow

And raises me near to Thy breast
And brings my anxious soul to rest
And hides me with Thy covering wings
To make my heart Thy praises sing

When I have need, then Thou art there
When I have want, then Thou dost share
The exceeding riches of Thy grace
The absolute beauty of Thy face
There is no other place to go
No other love my heart would know
But Thine alone! But Thine alone!
In Thee... I am at home

O Mighty Lifter of my day
Who swiftly moves to guard my way
What peace when life is in Thine hands
A mystery man can't understand
For when my heart with fear is filled
Thou speaks and makes the storms be still
And whispers soft till sleep is sweet
Even in the bowels of the angry deep

Thus when the day breaks, I too shall rise
With lifted face unto Thy skies
With lifted hands and lifted heart
To exalt Thy name for how great Thou art
Yes, this heart accepts Thy sacrifice
Sweet exchange of death for everlasting life
Sweet exchange of night for never-ending day
Evermore to behold my Redeemer's face

So lift up thy head and be glad my soul
For the Lord thy God hast made thee whole
O clap thy hands and with praise rejoice
For thine ear hast heard her Beloved's voice
O "bless the Lord O my soul and all that is within"
The First, the Last, the Here and Now, the Beginning and the End
O bless the Lord all the earth for the rich bounties He imparts
O bless His name, Jehovah; He is the Lifter of our hearts

O I bless Thy name, Jehovah, O Thou Sweet Lifter of *my* Heart!

November 23, 2013

(Dedicated to my brother, Chris)

*O taste and see that the Lord is good: blessed is the
man that trusteth in Him. (Psalm 34:8, KJV)*

*Bless the Lord, O my soul: and all that is within me,
bless His holy name. (Psalm 103:1, KJV)*

My Heart Is Full!

Thou hast made known to me the ways of life; Thou shalt make me full of joy with Thy countenance. —Act 2:28 (KJV)

I hear the anguish in disheartened voices filled with woe
Not knowing what to do or where to go
Hearts marked with emptiness
Consumed in hopelessness
And I search for words that will make their hearts to know
That only God can give new life to dying souls

For I, too, was a prisoner of the dark and only knew of night
And the master whom I served deceived me with his lies
Still, I thought that life was great
And was content to live "my way"
Until I found myself alone, forsaken, lost
Until I found myself prostrate beneath His Cross

But then... God broke those chains of iron and made me to be free!
He cut the bars asunder for He hast pardoned me
From hell's dungeon I've been claimed
And I no longer am the same
For I now live in the countenance of His face
I now bask in the radiance of His grace

Today my heart is full because of Christ
He "hast made known to me the ways of life"
I give praise for all He hast done for me
And know there is nothing quite as sweet
As the pure beauty of His love that woos my heart
And the sweetness of His voice that makes it throb...

My heart is full! My heart is full! For Thou hast made it so!
Heaven and Earth cannot contain the splendor of Thy love
Even in sleep I too rejoice
For I know sweet slumber at Thy voice

As I am sheltered safe in the warm embrace of my Most Beloved
O I bless The Lord Jehovah; for His name is Wonderful!

For He is merciful forever
True and righteous altogether
Holds me up with His right hand
Makes my staggering feet to stand
Gives me rest and sweet repose
Even while the storm wind blows
He blesses those who would bless me
Contends with those who contend with me
He wields all power, strength and might
For He, Himself, takes up the fight
And parts the sea with mighty hands
To make my feet to walk dry land
In the fiery furnace, He is at my side
The consuming flames are neutralized
As His massive wings around me fold
O He greatly saves to the uttermost
And in the den where the lions feast
He shuts the mouths of the ferocious beasts
Then spreads a table just for me
Yes, even "in the presence of mine enemies"
He feeds my soul with tenderness
Then leads me on with gentleness
The loving Shepherd ever giving
Wonderfully gracious and abundantly forgiving
His countenance shines upon the upright
For in His presence is joy and delight
In His presence is glory and majesty
In His presence is deliverance and victory

Who is this mighty King of Kings
Who freely gives to us all things?
It is Jehovah, the Most High God
Who saved my soul at Calvary's cross
He fills me up with all that's good
He fills *me* up with all that's good
He fills me up with *all* that's good
Indeed, my heart is full!

Truly... God will shower you with goodness; it will take your breath away
He will shine His face upon you; you will bask beneath His rays
Even now He bids "come home"
And yearns and pleas for you to come
Why not walk into the fortress of this great and awesome love
And be made to shout with gladness! "O my heart is full!
O my soul rejoice for The Lord hast made me full!
O rejoice my soul for indeed my heart is full!"

August 2, 2014

(Dedicated, with special affection, to Pastor and Sister James Gbolo)

For the righteous Lord loveth righteousness; His countenance doth behold the upright. (Psalm 11:7, KJV)

Oh that men would praise the Lord for His goodness, and for His wonderful works to the children of men! (Psalm 107:8, KJV)

The Lord is my shepherd; I shall not want.
He maketh me to lie down in green pastures:
He leadeth me beside the still waters. He restoreth my soul:
He leadeth me in the paths of righteousness for His name's sake.
Yea, though I walk through the valley of the shadow of death, I will fear
no evil: for Thou art with me; Thy rod and Thy staff they comfort me.
Thou preparest a table before me in the presence of mine enemies:
Thou anointest my head with oil; my cup runneth over.
Surely goodness and mercy shall follow me all the days of my life:
and I will dwell in the house of the Lord for ever. (Psalm 23, KJV)

Never Forget

Bless the Lord, O my soul, and forget not all His benefits.
—Psalm 103:2 (KJV)

When at last the day is done
And I recline with the setting sun
There I find sweet solitude
And feel such peace alone with You
But ofttimes in the midst of day
Cluttered with things to do and say
I soon forget to say a prayer
And no longer regard Your loving care
The hours travel swiftly by
Only to find I have left Your side

But then there's days when in my heart
I never feel Your presence part
The joy You placed within my soul
Makes me full and takes control
And in every thought and every deed
I find myself praising Thee—
Yes, grateful for my God above!
Most thankful for His selfless love!
Glad that through His piercing death
He hast brought me to Himself

O bless the Lord, O my soul! Let not my heart forget—
Thy love, Thy tenderest mercies—the *full* of all Thy benefits

November 1977

Bless the Lord, O my soul, and forget not all His benefits:
Who forgiveth all thine iniquities;
Who healeth all thy diseases;
Who redeemeth thy life from destruction;
Who crowneth thee with lovingkindness and tender mercies;
Who satisfieth thy mouth with good things;
so that thy youth is renewed like the eagle's.
The Lord executeth righteousness and judgment for
all that are oppressed. (Psalm 103:2–6, KJV)

None Like Thee

Remember the former things of old: for I am God, and there is none else;
I am God, and there is none like Me. —Isaiah 46:9 (KJV)

At the hearing of Thy voice
My heart grows full
As I taste the utter sweetness
Of Thy gracious love
Savoring well Thy richly gifts
Thy warmth and tenderness
And all within me smiles
For I am truly blessed!

Yet, at the thunder of Thy voice
The woeful earth upheaves
Leveling mountains and hilltops
And arousing angry seas
As the cruel and treacherous waves
Pursue death by watery grave
Thy love in perfect form makes haste
Thy trembling child to save

For truly there is none other
Who is likened unto Thee
Who can ride the winds of storms
Just to set His people free
For the battle alone is His
And thusly He shall fight
O Thou Most Fearsome Warrior
And too my Shining Knight
There is none—indeed not one
Who is quite like Thee!

At the bending of Thine ear
A prayer is heard
And caught up is every groan
And every word
To the bosom of Thine heart
Where none can grasp or tear apart
The expectations of the child
Whose hope is bound in Thee

Yet... the bending of Thine ear
Gives pause to some
Whose hearts are bent on evil
And would Thy children overcome
Wicked whisperings are fed
To hungry ears of the breathing dead
As the child of God is sorely tried
Almost more than she can bear

But then lo and behold! My Deliverer!
O what other can be likened unto Thee!
Who flashes down from Heaven
In just a blinking of the eye
And obliterates the storms
Defies the darkness of the skies
For the battle alone is His
And thusly He shall fight
O Thou Formidable Warrior
and too my Fairest Knight
There is none—indeed not one
Who is quite like Thee!

At the pounding of the nails
He sees *my* face
With His pained and wounded hands
I am embraced

As the falling of His precious blood
Covers me in unrequited love
This Wondrous Savior conquers *all* to rescue me
No, there is no one who is likened unto Thee!

The Lion and the Lamb
Truly Thou art
Invincible Warrior, Immaculate Savior
O Thou Champion of my Heart
Thy strength hast made Thee Great
Thy gentleness, adored
Thou who speaks in a still small voice
Doth thunders and rumbles and roars
What stealth! Yet astounding Majesty!
With such hands that never tire
Sometimes with softness in Thy touch
Sometimes with eyes of fire!
Thou places dread in the hearts of men
But Thine love *my* heart dost melt
O, there is no one who is quite like Thee
Thou art God and no one else!

Hear ye, fear ye the Everlasting!
As lightning and thunder, breaking mountains, rocks and trees
As *He* declares: "I am God, and there is none else!
I am God, and there is *none* like Me!"

October 21, 2017

And, behold, the Lord passed by, and a great and strong wind rent the mountains, and brake in pieces the rocks before the Lord; but the Lord was not in the wind: and after the wind an earthquake; but the Lord was not in the earthquake: And after the earthquake a fire; but the Lord was not in the fire: and after the fire a still small voice. (1 Kings 19:11–12, KJV)

For who in the Heaven can be compared unto the Lord? who among the sons of the mighty can be likened unto the Lord? (Psalm 89:6, KJV)

Sacrifice of Praise!

My soul doth magnify the Lord, and my spirit hath rejoiced in God my Savior. For He that is mighty hath done to me great things.
—Luke 1:46–47, 49 (KJV)

Therefore let us offer the sacrifice of praise to God continually, that is, the fruit of our lips giving thanks to His name. —Hebrews 13:15 (KJV)

Father, how do I say thank you
for it seems each time I try
the tears at once begin to well
beneath my bended brow
for Thou hast heard from Heaven
and hast attended to our prayers
and the need that sorely pressed our hearts
Thou hast brought beneath Thy care

And how sweetly Thou hast intervened
in this desperate time of need
when at Thy Throne of Grace we bowed
seeking help from none, but Thee
And our humbled faith found favor
from Thee, the King of Kings
Thou hast kindly lifted up our heads
and made our hearts to sing

And thus, my Lord, what can I say
that is worthy of Thine ears
I search in vain to find such words
but they only come in tears
And so I'll let my praise flow out
in exaltation Lord to Thee
Accept these droplets of my love
for Thou hast honored me!

And may these tears of gratitude
my most grateful praise to Thee
ascend unto Thy Holy Throne
and fall upon Thy feet
And like Mary, may I too reflect
an all-consuming love for Thee
with tears that bathe in silent praise
for what Thou hast done for me

And soon one day with perfect eyes
I shall look upon Thy face
My lips in adoration
shall shout with perfect praise
And the tears that I had thought one day
would surely cease to flow
shall pour out in waves of gratefulness
for the mercies Thou hast shown

Yes Lord, these tears upon my face
are but a sacrifice of praise
They are the firstfruits of my stammering lips
Giving thanks unto Thy name!
They are offerings made by fire
a sweet savor unto Thee
O my soul dost magnify Thy name
for Thou hast done a great thing for me!

Yes! "My soul doth magnify the Lord
and my spirit hath rejoiced...
for He that is mighty"
will do great things for us!

February 26, 2014

(Dedicated to my brother, Roy)

The Object of My Praise!

I will bless the Lord at all times: His praise shall continually be in my mouth. My soul shall make her boast in the Lord: the humble shall hear thereof, and be glad. —Psalm 34:1-2 (KJV)

Great is the Lord, and greatly to be praised!" —Psalm 48:1 (KJV)

Surely you have not known love
until God becomes the object of your praise
for His ears are ever open to the penitent cry
before you call, He hast made a way to provide
and hast searched the whole earth to and fro
traversing the abyss of hell's black abode
into turbulent seas and its merciless waves
shifting and shaping the inevitable grave
until He who masters the infamous seas
rebukes its power and the waters retreat
then under His feathers He covers you
with healing in His wings, He restores anew

Albeit a storm or violent night
or rather the dawn of Heaven's light
O it matters not *where* He leads the way—
for still... out of the depths of your heart you will say
"O hail Thee! Hallelujah! My Beloved and My Praise!"

Truly you have not lived
until God becomes the object of your praise
and you rest upon His bosom sweet
holding dear to your heart every word He speaks
beholding the beauty of His glorious face
treasuring each moment of His warm embrace
He refreshes with soothing waves of joy
quenching your wanting, thirsty soul

'til the dry parched ground beneath your feet
gives way to rolling hills of green
with fragrant gardens and sweet delights
unfolding still in the midst of night
and sweeter yet in the light of day
when His goodness comes out to play

Albeit cool waters to restore and refresh
or maybe, instead, a lone wilderness
O it matters not *where* He leads the way—
for still... out of the depths of your heart you will say
O hail Thee! Hallelujah! My Beloved and My Praise!

Acquaint yourself now with Him
This is where new life begins
that your burdens may be relieved
that your children, too, may know of His peace
God holds before you today... death and life
cursing and blessings herein doth lie
O choose wisely the goodly part
that no one can take away—
that is, sit at the feet of Jesus
fall in love with Him every day
His love awakes love, and your heart will reside
beyond the dark clouds of Earth's tainted skies
unto the rich dwellings of a heavenly place
unto the sweet bosom of He Who Saves
and there from a most grateful heart you will say
"O Lord, Thou art worthy of all praise!"
as the angels join in with melodious refrain
"Worthy of all power, riches and wisdom
Worthy of all honor and glory and blessings
Unto Him that sitteth on the Throne
and to the Lamb to whom all praises belong!"

O "Worthy is the Lamb that was slain!"
Let us be glad and rejoice in His name!

Behold now the Throne of the Ancient of Days
and worship Him, The Creator, the Embodiment of Praise
Most Reverend and Holy is His Majesty's name
O hail Thee! Hallelujah! My Beloved and My Praise!

I hail Thee! Hallelujah!
"For the Lord God Omnipotent reigns!"

January 7, 2020

And Jesus answered and said unto her, "Martha, Martha, thou art careful and troubled about many things: But one thing is needful: and Mary hath chosen that good part, which shall not be taken away from her." (Luke 10:41–42, KJV)

Acquaint now thyself with Him, and be at peace: thereby good shall come unto thee. (Job 22:21, KJV)

I call Heaven and Earth to record this day against you, that I have set before you life and death, blessing and cursing: therefore choose life, that both thou and thy seed may live. (Deuteronomy 30:19, KJV)

And I heard, as it were, the voice of a great multitude, as the sound of many waters and as the sound of mighty thunderings, saying, "Alleluia! For the Lord God Omnipotent reigns!" (Revelation 19:6, NKJV)

Saying with a loud voice, "Worthy is the Lamb that was slain to receive power, and riches, and wisdom, and strength, and honour, and glory, and blessing." And every creature which is in Heaven, and on the Earth, and under the Earth, and such as are in the sea, and all that are in them, heard I saying, "Blessing, and honour, and glory, and power, be unto Him that sitteth upon the throne, and unto the Lamb for ever and ever."
(Revelation 5:12–13, KJV)

What Shall I Render?

What shall I render unto the Lord for all His benefits toward me? I will take the cup of salvation, and call upon the name of the Lord. I will pay my vows unto the Lord now in the presence of all His people.
—Psalm 116:12–14 (KJV)

Honor the Lord with thy substance and with the firstfruits of all thine increase. —Proverbs 3:9 (KJV)

The Lord hast brought me to a better place
Quite far from where I started from
And the life that I now live in Jesus
Is anchored in His everlasting arms
For He heard when I cried to the heavens
And He reached down to that dark pit of hell
Raised me swiftly to the warmth of His bosom
And all my pain and fears were expelled

Yes, He hast brought me to a much better place
Though there are times when the tears still flow
Not because of a troubled and a downcast heart
It is because He hast loved me so
For He is gracious in kindness and mercy
And wields the strength of His power just for me
I am still quite amazed that the touch of His hand
In a moment made all storms to cease

And what I now know of my Wonderful Savior
Far exceeds all this heart would desire
To think I once doubted the strength of His love
And refused to believe in its power

It is true, there's no other who makes life complete
There's no other who is fairer than He
For He is great in His mercies and abundant in blessings
And hast given more than my heart can receive

He hast given me much! He hast forgiven me much!
O this debt of love I can never repay
So what shall I render unto the Blessed Redeemer
For all the benefits His hand sends my way
In the presence of His people, I will now give Him praise
And return to Him all that I owe
The firstfruits of my labor, the firstfruits of my increase
For these are fruits of the love He bestows

One day soon I shall see Him in all of His glory
One day soon I'll spread wings and take flight
I shall journey with Jesus and the host of His angels
From Earth's darkness to Eternal Light
O I shall follow the Lamb whithersoever He goeth
For from death unto life I've been raised
O how my heart will adore Him as I bow down before Him
Tendering offerings of thanksgiving and praise

But what now shall I render unto my Gracious Redeemer
For all the goodness His love doth provide
I shall take the sweet cup of salvation
And return what *His* hand hath supplied
The first of my love, the first of my praise
The first of the fruits of the land
For the windows of Heaven are now pouring rich blessings
From His gracious and bountiful hands!

O Yes! Infinite blessings! Exceeding great blessings!
Immeasurable, incredible, resplendent!
He invites us to prove the full depths of His love
O "there shall not be room enough to receive it"

May 10, 2014

Prove me now herewith, saith the Lord of hosts, if I will not open you the windows of Heaven, and pour you out a blessing, that there shall not be room enough to receive it. (Malachi 3:10, KJV)

Faith

and

Trust

Faith and trust in God is of paramount importance. For "without faith it is impossible to please Him: for he that cometh to God must believe that He is, and that He is a rewarder of them that diligently seek Him" (Hebrews 11:6, KJV). We have faith in God because we know who He is and what He can do. We trust God because we have full confidence that He will do for us what He has promised. In all areas of our lives—our homes, our jobs, our churches and our communities—our every expectation should be in God, and God alone. Man cannot save us. We cannot save ourselves, nor can we save others. But thanks be to God, Jesus saves! Therefore, we shall wait upon our God, because our expectations are in Him.

Expectations

My soul, wait thou only upon God; for my expectation is from Him.
—Psalm 62:5 (KJV)

O how the enemy my soul doth try
He seems to press on every side
'Tis true he prowls the midnight hour
Seeking whom he may devour
Ofttimes in trusted friends he strikes
Misled by charm and twisted lies
And how the heart aches heavily
When a friend succumbs to his deceit
And though we try with finite hands
To mend their hearts to understand
What painful loss that leaves a hole
When darkness takes control
O Blessed Father Thou hast taught me well
Thy hands *alone* can never fail
As such, I pray and dare not cease
For my expectations are from Thee

O how the wicked stirs up strife
To those who would partake of life
They cast dark shadows, spread false truths
With words like arrows, sharp yet smooth
But truth and knowledge is in Thine hands
And thus I look to Thee, not man
For it matters not what they believe
When the God of love hast befriended me
What ugly hate Thine heart endured
Just to make my redemption sure
The devil constant to Thy side
To thwart the plans for which You died

And yet the Father's strength You prayed
Though pained the path, You did not stray
Our meager trials cannot compare
To the agony You chose to bear
Though persecuted, yet You forgave
Though dying, the dying thief You saved
Such perfect love brings me to shame
When with selfish pride I deny Your name
Remind me of Your pain and loss
Your wounded hands on Calvary's cross
For Thou hast suffered all for me
That Thou may bless in abundancy

All Heaven's riches from Thee flow
That love for Thee may deeper grow
That faith may prosper and increase
Just look what Thou hast done for me
From the shadow of death, I now have life
From the depths of hell, to Paradise
From hopelessly lost, to assuredly found
I am no longer a captive; I have been unbound
All that I have committed to Thee
Thou hast proven that Thou art able to keep
"For I am persuaded that neither death nor life"
Will separate me from the love of Christ
Though afflicted, my voice still sings Thy praise
Though cast down, with joy my heart is raised
Though slain by Thee, I still shall trust
For faith awaits Thy healing touch

And thus when tears disturb my sleep
It is *Thy* face alone I seek
I look to *Thee* to attend my needs
I look to *Thee* to deliver me

When at the cross my heart bends low
I expect *Thy* fount to overflow
Though all may cast a doubtful eye
I have set my face unto Thy skies

And so my woeful heart may mourn
When from love's arm a friend is torn
In Thy safe arms there is comfort sweet
Strong arms that won't let go of me
So I hasten to Thy Throne of Grace
For my soul hast need to see Thy face
And as my tears fall at Thy feet
I look to Thee, *expectantly*

I am assured the blessing that I seek
"For I know in whom I have believed"
The Most High God who never sleeps
Is the God whose ear inclines to me
My desires, Lord, are in Thine hands
Holy angels await at Thy command
And sweet Thy blessings they shall release
Because...
My expectations are in Thee

June 13, 2013

For I know whom I have believed, and am persuaded that He is able to keep that which I have committed unto Him. (2 Timothy 1:12, KJV)

For I am persuaded, that neither death, nor life, nor angels, nor principalities, nor powers, nor things present, nor things to come, nor height, nor depth, nor any other creature, shall be able to separate us from the love of God, which is in Christ Jesus our Lord. (Romans 8:38–39, KJV)

Guardian of Israel: Psalm 121

*I will lift up mine eyes unto the hills, from whence cometh my help.
My help cometh from the Lord, which made Heaven and Earth.
—Psalm 121:1–2 (KJV)*

*I will lift mine eyes on high
Beyond the hilltops and the mountains
Unto the source of strength and life
Unto Jehovah God, the Creator
The Father of Heaven and Earth
O the Gracious Keeper of my soul
For my help, my strength, my comfort
Comes from the Lord*

*He will continually guard thy steps
Not allowing thy foot to stumble or slip
For behold, The Sweet Guardian of Israel
He neither dozes, nor does He sleeps
When the sun would surely smite thee
God is thy shade, thy protection and shield
And when darkness and evil pursues thee
By His right hand, the foe is stilled*

*O The Lord will preserve thy soul
He will guard thy going outs and thy coming ins
"From this time forth, and even for evermore"
Thou art safe when thine eyes are on Him*

Thou art safe in My Beloved Elohim

July 12, 2018

(Dedicated to Pastor & Sister Rohan Simpson)

I will lift up mine eyes unto the hills, from whence cometh my help.
My help cometh from the Lord, which made Heaven and Earth.
He will not suffer thy foot to be moved: He that keepeth thee will not slumber.
Behold, He that keepeth Israel shall neither slumber nor sleep.
The Lord is thy keeper: the Lord is thy shade upon thy right hand.
The sun shall not smite thee by day, nor the moon by night.
The Lord shall preserve thee from all evil: He shall preserve thy soul.
The LORD shall preserve thy going out and thy coming in
from this time forth, and even for evermore.
(Psalm 121:1–8, KJV)

Hope Thou in God

Why art thou cast down, O my soul? and why art thou disquieted within me? hope thou in God: for I shall yet praise Him, who is the health of my countenance, and my God. —Psalm 42:11 (KJV)

Tell me why, O my soul, are ye discouraged
Why is thine anxious heart so troubled and afraid
Art thou not the favored child of God Almighty
Who hath redeemed thee... yes, even from the grave
For the Lord thy God, hitherto, hast helped thee
He is The Deliverer, and, too, thy Beloved and Faithful Friend
And though this vicious foe pursues with unrelenting forces
Thou hast a God who saveth still with mighty hands

Therefore, my soul, be reminded of His goodness
Be thou reminded, He is gracious unto thee
For God, Himself, hath hitherto delivered
From the storms of night unto the light of eternity

Why art thou cast down, O my soul, and disheartened?
Is there not a God in Israel who will fight for thee this day?
Who is great in lovingkindness and full in tender mercies
Whose help hath marked the countenance of thy face
In all life's trials, albeit the most perplexed of situations
God hast promised "as thy days, so shall thy strength be"
"Let not your heart be troubled" for you are e'er before His presence
For the precious blood of His dear Son still covers, even thee

Hast thou forgotten *thy* fiery furnace of affliction?
Hast thou forgotten *thy* Red Sea or the mighty lion's roar?
For God delivered greatly, and thine heart did greatly praise Him
And thou shalt praise Him yet again, O my soul, forevermore!

Hope thou in God, and thy faith shall be rewarded
Hope thou in God, O Thou Wondrous Counselor
Hope thou in God, and thou shalt only live to praise Him
Thou shalt surely praise Him yet again! O my soul, forevermore!

O Thou shalt love Him greatly! O yes my soul! Yes, my soul, forevermore!

April 25, 2017

And as thy days, so shall thy strength be. (Deuteronomy 33:25, KJV)

Then Samuel took a stone, and set it between Mizpeh and Shen, and called the name of it Eben-ezer, saying, Hitherto hath the Lord helped us. (1 Samuel 7:12, KJV)

Peace I leave with you, My peace I give unto you: not as the world giveth, give I unto you. Let not your heart be troubled, neither let it be afraid. (John 14:27, KJV)

I Have Set My Love on Him: Psalm 91

He that dwelleth in the secret place of the Most High shall abide under the shadow of the Almighty. Because he hath set his love upon Me, therefore will I deliver him: I will set him on high, because he hath known My name. He shall call upon Me, and I will answer him: I will be with him in trouble; I will deliver him, and honour him. With long life will I satisfy him, and shew him My salvation. —Psalm 91:1, 14–16 (KJV)

Because I have set my love on Him
A promise to me hast been made
The terror by night and arrow by day
No longer can make me afraid
For under the shadow of the Almighty wings
I rest in His infinite care
For I have made the Most High my dwelling place
And I am kept from the enemy's snare

He hast given His angels charge over me
To keep me in all of His ways
They shall bear me up lest I stumble and fall
By their hands, my steps are made safe
For the Lord is my refuge and fortress
In Him will I trust all my days
And thus, no evil shall befall me
Because I know His name

I have set my love on my Father
And He hast promise to set me on high
A thousand shall fall all around me
But as for me, it shall not come nigh
For He covers me with His feathers
And under His wings I trust
Mine eyes shall behold the wicked's reward
And be made glad for the cause of the just

Because I have set my love on Him
My Father will honor me
In trouble, I'll hasten to call on His name
And a mighty deliverer He'll be
O He will show me His salvation
And my soul shall be satisfied
For His blessings are sweetest to those that dwell
In the secret place of the Most High

March 24, 2012

(Dedicated to Joslynn, Nadia, and Myles and to the loving memory of Sis. Ruth Ward)

For He shall give His angels charge over thee, to keep thee in all thy ways. (Psalm 91:11, KJV)

I Know The King!

God is our refuge and strength, a very present help in trouble.
—Psalm 46:1 (KJV)

Sometimes the winds of life blow hard upon this soul of mine
It seems the storm looms greater, and the calm is hard to find
The thunder sounds a threatening voice
Giving pause to everything
But it's okay... and I'm alright
You see, I know the King

There are days when those around me seek to cause my hurt and pain
And they draw their swords against me; they conspire against my name
Their well-laid plans are masterful
But they forget just this one thing
That the Most High God
Is my dwelling place
You see, I know the King

He hast promised me He will never leave for a moment, nor forsake
And His eyes are watching over me, guarding every step I take
And when I approach His royal throne
To make known my request
The King holds out His scepter
And grants me all I ask

Thus, I have no need for worry, no reason to fear or dread
For God is my defender, and He will do what He hath said
Why is my heart so joyful?
Why do His praise I sing?
Because I am the favored daughter
Of Jesus Christ, the King

So whatever it is the enemy may whisper in your ear
He has no power over me; my Present Help is here
I am God's prized possession
And I am safe beneath His wings
The enemy *is* defeated!
Praise God, I know the King!

June 14, 2012

(To Karen)

More of Thee!

Delight thyself also in the Lord; and He shall give thee the desires of thine heart. —Psalm 37:4 (KJV)

A New Year's Prayer

Heavenly Father, Thou hast promised to abundantly bless
To forgive and to cleanse and to restore righteousness
That I might serve Thee alone with a perfect heart
And come before Thy presence, unblemished, unmarred
Make me to know Thee and to walk true to Thy ways
To inquire of Thy wisdom and to quickly obey
For the enemy doth sway me to bend to the night
Make haste to Thy servant and defend what is Thine

Thou hast promised the desires of my heart shall be mine
And I await now before Thee and beg all that is Thine
For the things of this world are now foreign and strange
Thus I cleave to Thee, Father, till Thine heart I have claimed
More of Thee, all of Thee, only Thee is my desire
To be consumed by Thy love, to be filled with Thy power
To receive of Thy spirit and its rich blessings impart
To be covered and sheltered, bound close to Thine heart

Until that day when Michael the Great Prince shall stand
To make sure our deliverance out of enemy hands
He shall come in the clouds with His chariots of fire
With His myriads of angels in royal splendor and power
O my Lord come Thou quickly; make short these last days
That our eyes may behold the glorious beauty of Thy face

We shall shout praise continually throughout the realms of all eternity
But the lips of this grateful heart shall utter still in tender whisperings—
"More of Thee, O my Blessed Redeemer!
More of Thee! All of Thee! Only Thee!
More of Thee, Thou Beloved Gracious Savior!
This lowly heart hath but one desire... Lord, more of Thee!"

October 3, 2014

(Dedicated to Sis. Michelle Thomas)

My Plans for You

For I know the thoughts that I think toward you, saith the Lord, thoughts of peace, and not of evil. —Jeremiah 29:11 (KJV)

"These are *their* plans for you My child... not Mine"
The Father wakes me gently and in love doth reprimand
"I would that thou had come to Me instead
and thou would find sweet rest upon thy bed
Cease now this tossing to and fro of wearied mind
See how the enemy baits thee with casting of the line
Had thou inquired of Me, thou surely would have seen
their thoughts are not My thoughts
their ways are far from Me

"Place thy trust in Me alone, O child of anxious heart
Lean on Me and all thy ways I shall jealously regard
for every step of thine is ordered from above
that thou may know full measure of the sweetness of My love
for I know the plans I have for you; they are full of peace
of lovingkindness, tender mercies and love that will not cease
Seek now My face that thou may dwell in My eternal light
and I will keep thy feet always in the path that leads to life"

Straightway I fall, O Precious Christ, upon Thy nail-scarred feet
Forgive and cleanse my wanting soul of all that displeases Thee
for I know, O Lord, the way of man is not within himself
"It is not in man that walketh to direct his steps"
The place that hast been set for me indeed is not Thine own
for they discerneth not, O Lord, to whom my heart belongs
Although I faltered greatly in not seeking out Thy will
Thou hast sought me out in tenderness to direct my pathway still

O give me such a heart, O Lord, that cannot turn from Thee
for Thy wondrous love and kindness doth attend my every need
As such, my heart shall ever seek the bending of Thy face
that Thou may find sweet pleasure in my offerings of praise

And on that day when mine eyes shall see the home Thou hast prepared
and my feet shall touch the golden streets of Jerusalem so splendrously fair
may I hear Thy whisper in my ear:
"Behold, beloved, *My* plan—not theirs"
And mine eyes shall behold eternity...
the gift of Thy sweet love for me
not marked by days or weeks or years
but in time everlasting... where there are no tears
This was *Thy* plan right from the start
that we be with Thee where Thou art
to share in the joy of our Savior and Lord
in the vast, glorious, untainted realms
of *Happily Ever After*...
Forevermore!

August 16, 2019

O Lord, I know that the way of man is not in himself: it is not in man
that walketh to direct his steps. (Jeremiah 10:23, KJV)

My Soul Yearns for Thee

So I find it to be a law that when I want to do right, evil lies close at hand. For I delight in the law of God, in my inner being, but I see in my members another law waging war against the law of my mind and making me captive to the law of sin that dwells in my members. Wretched man that I am! Who will deliver me from this body of death? —Romans 7:21–24 (ESV)

But my eyes are fixed on You, O God... In You I seek refuge; do not leave my soul defenseless. —Psalm 141:8 (BSB)

The struggle rages still on and on
and I most wretched, tired and worn
an unflinching enemy I now fight
the greater foe, though not from without
but against what lies within
an exasperating conflict...
that knows no end

What does one do
when the battle against oneself
is fraught with endless fails
scattered, shattered victories
all triumphs ending in defeat
and hope that crashes yet again
a daunting, unrelenting war...
I cannot win

And yet my deepest fear
that weighs heavy in the night
it is not this seeming, hopeless fight
but that I would somehow from the fall
no longer hear Your call
no longer yearn for Thee
rejecting entrance to Thy Throne
where Thou in tenderest love awaits
to save mightily Thine own

But even so, my Lord
I lift up mine eyes to Thee
Although my soul remains athirst
my unsung praises shall be heard
for when I stumble in the dark
Thou standeth near, and not afar
Thy lovely form doth bend and seek
all hearts whose eyes are fixed on Thee
this heart whose eyes are fixed on Thee

O my soul doth yearn for Thee, O Christ!
My soul yearns still for Thee!

October 30, 2018

As the deer pants for streams of water, so my soul pants for You, my God.
My soul thirsts for God, for the living God. (Psalm 42:1–2, NIV)

Promised Spirit

*But when the Comforter is come, whom I will send unto you from the Father,
even the Spirit of Truth, which proceedeth from the Father, He shall testify
of Me. —John 15:26 (KJV)*

Promised Spirit of Heavenly Power
Breathe now upon these hearts of ours
We pray for Thy presence to dwell within
Be Thou our guide, our unfailing friend
Bathe us in excellent love for truth
To quicken, convict and reprove
With Thy passion and fervor, revive us again
Come forth as the mightiest of winds

Beloved Comforter, the Empowering One
Christ's parting words assured You would come
We now seek Thy boundless resources of grace
We ask Thee for showers in fathomless waves
For Thou *will* restore hearts again
Convicting the souls of lost men
As our stuttering tongues speak eloquent
In the power of the Heavenly Sent

For no human wisdom though greatly learned
Can make Thy truths to be discerned
And no logic or reason can touch the souls
Of those whose hearts have grown hard and cold
It will not be by strength, neither by might
Nor how great we can pray or hard we can fight
When the *Spirit* is come, "Ye shall then receive power"
With a mighty unveiling in Earth's final hours

Thus Sweet Holy Spirit descend from above
Pour greatly upon us Thy abundance of love
May The Lord Crucified be the Prince of our lives
May we live for His glory, may our tongues testify

Of His goodness, His grace, of His merciful ways
Of His excellence in power and His worthiness of praise
Let the Sword of the Spirit pierce its way through our hearts
As the sweet saving Truth to the world we impart

For when "He, the Spirit of Truth is come"
He will make plain the path to our heavenly home
Soon Christ shall descend and His children will rise
To meet our dear King in the brightest of skies
O what joy it shall be when our Savior we see
O what joy, yes indeed, when Christ sees you and me
He shall shout with a joy that none other hast known
"Come, ye blessed of my Father! Thou art home!"
"Come, ye blessed of my Father! Thou art home!"

May 16, 2013

Howbeit when He, the Spirit of Truth, is come, He will guide you into all truth. (John 16:13, KJV)

*Come ye blessed of My Father, inherit the kingdom prepared for you
from the foundation of the world. (Matthew 25:34, KJV)*

Stormy Voices

O God of our salvation; who art the confidence of all the ends of the Earth, and of them that are afar off upon the sea: Which by His strength setteth fast the mountains; being girded with power: Which stilleth the noise of the seas, the noise of their waves, and the tumult of the people.
—Psalm 65:5–7 (KJV)

So many voices within, dear Lord
I hear the screams and the shouts
Calling me, pulling me, pushing and shoving me
With increasingly thunderous howls
But Thou art the Master of the turbulent seas
Belligerent tides retreat on command
When girded in strength, O Thou King of the Earth
Raise high Thy most powerful hands
And instantly, sweetly the waters obey
Thou hast silenced its monstrous roars
And perfectly stood the sea that day
As the waves caress softly the shore

So let it be with this heart of mine
When dark storms persistently rise
And the noises within so resoundingly rage
That this soul cannot hear her own cries
When the wrath of the waves would but swallow me whole
And the sea holds me under in fear
May I know—however ferocious the storm—
That my Master stands ready and near
Raise high Thy hand Lord! Raise high Thy hand!
Command the winds of this soul to be still
And Thy servant shall behold in all marvel and praise
As the storms bow down to Thy will

January 8, 1984

The floods have lifted up, O Lord, the floods have lifted up their voice; the floods lift up their waves. The Lord on high is mightier than the noise of many waters, yea, than the mighty waves of the sea. (Psalm 93:3–4, KJV)

There Is Nothing You Can Do to Me Today

What shall we then say to these things? If God be for us, who can be against us? He that spared not His own Son, but delivered Him up for us all, how shall He not with Him also freely give us all things?
—Romans 8:31–32 (KJV)

There is nothing you can do to me today
For I am in my Master's arms, and He is my constant stay
You may clip my wings, yet still I will arise and fly
Soaring upward and onward, beyond these cloudy skies
You may bind my feet, it matters not for I will surely fall
Into the arms of the Compassionate, who hears my every call
And by my Savior I shall stand
For my life is only in His hands
There is nothing you can do to me today

He knows the road I take for He, too, has gone before
And because I place my trust in Him, He blesses more and more
He stands behind the scenes of life and orders as He please
And yet from His throne on high, His ear inclines to me
You cannot know the peace that comes from resting in His care
For He, my Gracious Savior, bottles up my every tear
Heaven's Majesty is now my King
And I am safe beneath His sheltering wings
There is nothing you can do to me today

My Father is great in battle, mighty, terrible and fierce
Yet lovingly and tenderly He catches all my tears
And embraces me within His arms and holds me close and sure
A perfect rest amid the storms with mercies that endure
The enemy may assault with force that shatters, breaks and kills
But none can touch the soul who thus before the Father kneels
He is The Holy One
And I am covered though His Son
There is nothing you can do to me today

Yes, His bosom is my refuge, a loving, restful place
My life within His care is more than safe
For I live within the covenant of His abundant grace
There is nothing you can do to me today

March 31, 2011

(Dedicated to my brother, Vincent)

Voices of the Sea

And He said, "Come." And when Peter was come down out of the ship, he walked on the water, to go to Jesus. But when he saw the wind boisterous, he was afraid; and beginning to sink, he cried, saying, "Lord, save me." And immediately Jesus stretched forth His hand, and caught him.
—Matthew 14:29–31 (KJV)

O Lord, my God, I'm sinking fast
The billows are almost o'er me
The waves will have my soul at last
And plunge me beneath the sea
O Mighty God, my heart doth fear
The voices of the sea
As Thou delivered Peter
Please, Lord, deliver me

This raging tempest is too great
Beneath its waves I fall
Rescue!—before it is too late
Please save my storm-tossed soul
Thy voice that calms the mighty sea
Bring me to peaceful shore
I turn my weary eyes to Thee
Myself, I trust no more

The angry waters, the boisterous winds
May be my lot each day
Yet still my faith shall look to Thee
To guide my every way
Amid the storms, amid the waves
Amid the violent seas
The God, who delivered Peter
Shall, too, deliver me

December 9, 1979

Thou rulest the raging of the sea; when the waves thereof
arise, Thou stillest them. (Psalm 89:9, KJV)

Whom God Hath Blessed

God is not a man, that He should lie; neither the son of man, that He should repent: hath He said, and shall He not do it? or hath He spoken, and shall He not make it good? Behold, I have received commandment to bless: and He hath blessed; and I cannot reverse it.
—Numbers 23:19–20 (KJV)

My God is most wonderful
Far more than I understand
And I was so miserable
As He took my trembling hand
And brought me to His breast
Imparting such sweet rest
You cannot curse the child
Whom God hath blessed

My God is Lord and King
The ruler of my life
I looked to Him alone for strength
When dark the night
And to my bended side He pressed
And O my soul He hast caressed
You cannot curse the child
Whom God hath blessed

When He gives quietness
I will not troubled be
The center of the storm
Is where He shelters me
Though waves go crashing in
The storms, the mighty winds
Be quiet and be still!
For I am in His hands

O sweet and blessed thought
What then can make me fear?
Who then can taunt my soul
When God is here?
Thus in His care I rest
He giveth me what's best
You cannot curse the child
Whom God hath blessed

So Satan get behind
My Savior is afore
He is the "Great I Am"
The Loving Christ whom I adore
Though others greatly try
To cast their dreadful curse
What God Himself hath blessed
It cannot be reversed

Who then can curse the child
Whom God hath blessed!

March 6, 2011

(Dedicated to Gwen Baker)

When He giveth quietness, who then can make trouble? (Job 34:29, KJV)

With Thy Strength

O Lord, I am oppressed; undertake for me. —Isaiah 38:14 (KJV)

O Lord, my heart entreats Thine own
For my flesh indeed is weak
I pray that Thou would make me strong
For all power belongs to Thee
If Thy great and mighty hands
Would make haste my cause to undertake
Then my strength shall be renewed
And will be done for Thy name's sake
And I shall ride Thy chariots of fire
Unto Thy bosom there to dwell
And my heart would know no anguish
For Thou maketh all things well
And my desire, O Thou shall satisfy
With love as sweet as Thou art fair
Thy wondrous gifts make full my heart
As my weakness Thou dost bear
Hence, my soul is made impregnable
My beleaguered spirit free
Who then can stand against the child
Whose strength flows out of Thee

Though bent and sorely pressed, O Lord
Thy face my soul doth seek
This wicked foe desires my soul
But Thou hitherto hast prayed for me
And thus my love lays hold of Thine
As faith yields all to gracious hands
For God, Himself, will undertake
And make His staggering child to stand

With eagles' wings, my soul mounts up
Unto the stronghold of His care
The foe retreats at His command
Lo, this is how He answers prayer!
He kisses, too, my tears away
Removes all grievous stains
Then gifts me with a voice of praise
That I may celebrate His name

And I *will* celebrate Thy name
For Thou art God alone
For with bending love and everlasting arms
Thou hast made Thy strength mine own
And though a perfect heart I have yet to know
Of this one thing I am sure:
Thou art worthy, Lord, of the highest praise
And shall be praised forevermore!

Thou art worthy, Lord! Thou art worthy, Lord!
O Thou Beloved of Earth and of Heaven Adored!
Thou art worthy, Lord, of the highest praise!
And shall be praised forevermore!

O Thou shall be praised forevermore!

May 13, 2016

(Dedicated to Rosalyn Lightbourne Mingo)

And the Lord said, "Simon, Simon, behold, Satan hath desired to have you, that he may sift you as wheat: But I have prayed for thee, that thy faith fail not: and when thou art converted, strengthen thy brethren." (Luke 22:31–32, KJV)

Hast thou not known? hast thou not heard, that the everlasting God, the Lord, the Creator of the ends of the Earth, fainteth not, neither is weary? there is no searching of His understanding. He giveth power to the faint; and to them that have no might He increaseth strength. Even the youths shall faint and be weary, and the young men shall utterly fall: But they that wait upon the Lord shall renew their strength; they shall mount up with wings as eagles; they shall run, and not be weary; and they shall walk, and not faint. (Isaiah 40:28–31, KJV)

I will call upon the Lord, who is worthy to be praised: so shall I be saved from mine enemies. (Psalm 18:3, KJV)

Thou art worthy, O Lord, to receive glory and honour and power: for Thou hast created all things, and for Thy pleasure they are and were created. (Revelation 4:11, KJV)

Peace

and

Comfort

COMFORT ME • FOLLOW ME • I AM THY GOD • MY DWELLING PLACE
PEACEFUL WATERS • PERFECT PEACE • RETURN UNTO THY REST
SWEET MEDITATION • THE SECRET PLACE • THY FRAGRANCE SWEET
THY SLUMBER SHALL BE SWEET • UNTO THEE • WHY WEEPEST THOU?

There are many salutations in the Bible that include the word *peace*, and one of my favorites is found in 1 Samuel 25:6 (ESV): "Peace be to you, and peace be to your house, and peace be to all that you have." In this world of disquietude and division, I know what it is to have sleepless nights due to the anxieties and concerns of this world. But praise God, I also know what it is to rest perfect in the arms of my Beloved Christ, accepting His loving and gracious promises. King Solomon expressed one of these dear promises so beautifully in Proverbs 3:24, KJV: "When thou liest down, thou shalt not be afraid; yea, thou shalt lie down, and thy sleep shall be sweet." O what wondrous comfort! O what coveted peace!

Comfort Me

I will cry unto God Most High; unto God that performeth all things for me.
—Psalm 57:2 (KJV)

And He arose, and rebuked the wind, and said unto the sea, "Peace, be still." And the wind ceased, and there was a great calm. And they feared exceedingly, and said one to another, "What manner of man is this, that even the wind and the sea obey Him?" —Mark 4:39 & 41 (KJV)

O Blessed Father, sometimes it it hard to turn off the worry
Even though I know that Thou art even nearer than before
My troubled heart grows weary with uncertainties and conflicts
And I yearn that Thou wouldst ease the storm and guide me to peaceful shore
Thus, I lift my eyes unto Thine hills where my cries won't go unheeded
Thou will "make the storm a calm so that the waves thereof are still"
So men may know that Thou art God and with wonderment inquire
"What manner of man is this that even the wind and sea obeys His will?"

Reprove my unbelief that I might trust with calm assurance
For Thou who conquered even death holds all power in Thine hands
And the heart who rests beneath Thy care knows quietude and solace
Though the fiercest tempest shakes the very ground on which he stands
O release this anguish of my soul; I pray awake Thee now and save me
Take away all self-sufficiency that would sever me from Thee
Send forth Thy mightiest angels to encamp a guard about me
Lift up, O Lord, Thy countenance and bathe me in Thy peace

And I shall lift my voice in praise for the goodness Thou hast shown
For Thy wonderful works of mercy and lovingkindness to Thine own
Thou shall hear my cry from Heaven and will incline Thine ear toward me
Thou shall lift me out of my distress and perform "all things for me"

O I shall ever cry unto the God Most High, Thou who commands *this* raging sea
So that men may know it was indeed Thine hands that hast done a great thing for me!

October 19, 2015

Then they cry unto the Lord in their trouble, and He bringeth them out of their distresses. He maketh the storm a calm, so that the waves thereof are still. Oh that men would praise the Lord for His goodness, and for His wonderful works to the children of men! (Psalm 107:28–29, 31, KJV)

"Follow Me"

*And as Jesus passed forth from thence, He saw a man, named Matthew,
sitting at the receipt of custom: and He saith unto him, "Follow Me." And
he arose, and followed Him. —Matthew 9:9 (KJV)*

I hear His voice in the midnight hour
beckoning me to come
"Leave behind thy worldly cares
and take My hand and follow"
and I turn away from life's demands
and follow Christ instead
He leads me to His resting place
and upon His bosom, I lay my head...
and am kindly comforted

His words are sweet upon my ears
and His hand most soft upon my brow
and all concerns I leave behind
are most distant to me now
and I indeed would ever stay
in the beauty of this Eden place
the calm serene of nature's breeze
dancing flowers and lofty trees
and His fragrances of love
embracing me

O how my soul hast ever yearned
for this lovely garden treasure
its quietude and gentle grace
delights with wondrous pleasure
still... I entertain the thought:
"What if my feet should wander
and once again I'm lost"
and my countenance grows somber
but He assures me with His smile
as He smooths my bended brow

that He, a Gracious Father
will not forsake His child
and without a word, He takes my hand
and leads me tenderly to sleep
and I am ever grateful
that He hath made His place with me

Thus, whenever darkly shadows grow
and feed upon my wearied soul
I hear His voice in whispers say
"My child, where dost thou go?
Turn away and walk with Me
Those places are not meant for thee
follow only where I lead"
as He extends His loving hand
beckoning me again
and, yes, I follow Him

And if His way sometimes unfolds
in midst of dreadful storms
His hands doth guide my timid steps
as I trust and lean upon His arm
For I have truly come to know
that whithersoever my Father goes
His ways are perfect and blest
and will lead to His garden of rest
Yes, I hear Him now in tenderest plea
extending His hand of love to me
softly beckoning once again
"Child, follow thou Me?"
"O Thou knoweth well my Lord…
my heart shall follow Thee!"

April 26, 2019

(Dedicated to Jessica Beteta)

"I Am Thy God"

Fear thou not; for I am with thee: be not dismayed; for I am thy God: I will strengthen thee; yea, I will help thee; yea, I will uphold thee with the right hand of My righteousness. —Isaiah 41:10 (KJV)

*"This is the enemy
I am thy God"*

Those were the words I heard
clearly, distinctly
as I sat bent
thoroughly exasperated
and spent
grappling with an onslaught
of sharply bitter words
meant to pierce an already wounded heart

And I dearly long for peace
but it seems it's been so far removed
and the utter anguish of my soul
cannot be quieted
for I find myself confined
behind massive, towering bars of iron
shackled and scarred in chains that bind

*"This is the enemy
I AM THY GOD!"*

I hear those words again
though now in bolder tones
and with sudden, sure awareness
I understand
for I have walked this road before
I recognize these doors
and will certainly cross this sordid path again

for this *is* the enemy
for whom my heart doth loathe
this is who he is
this is what he does—
a swift, a fierce, a ruthless
destroyer of the soul!

But O the Lord my God Most Gracious
comes and sits close to my side
and with His words, He opens up my wearied ears and eyes:

"Fear thou not; for I am with thee:
be not dismayed; for I AM THY GOD:
I will strengthen thee;
yea, I will help thee;
yea, I will uphold thee
with the right hand of My righteousness"

"O Thou, my Sweet and Most Beloved
how can this be
that Thou wouldst hasten from Thy throne
to comfort me
and hast swept me to Thy bosom
at the onset of the storm
and all its devastation
Thou hast forborne"

My eyes swell up with tears
as I have found true rest
for in the covert of His sheltering wings
my dreadful cares are cast
for The Great "I Am Thy God"
upholds and strengthens me
and hast set me before His face
for always

O Blessed be Thy name, O God!
Blessed be Thy name!
Thou Magistrate over Heaven and Earth
doth overrule the intent of man
Thy praise shall stay upon my lips
as long as breath in me exists
through the endless ages of eternal bliss
O from everlasting... even unto everlasting!

Blessed be Thy name, O Lord!
Blessed be Thy name!

July 22, 2019

By this I know that Thou favourest me, because mine enemy doth not triumph over me. And as for me, Thou upholdest me in mine integrity, and settest me before Thy face for ever. Blessed be the Lord God of Israel from everlasting, and to everlasting. Amen, and Amen. (Psalm 41:11–13, KJV)

My Dwelling Place

Lord, Thou hast been our dwelling place in all generations.
—Psalm 90:1 (KJV)

I see it in their faces
their eyes
and their voices
as they walk unaware
as to whom their hearts belong
and sometimes find myself engaged
in the tainted conversations
taking on the sordid battles
that to me dost not belong

Lord, lift me up beyond the lures
of this swiftly dying world
unto the chambers of Thy bosom
where my soul will be preserved
remind me once again
as Thou hast done ofttimes before
that *Thou* hast been my dwelling place...
and shall be forevermore

June 20, 2019

*Cause me to hear Thy lovingkindness in the morning;
for in Thee do I trust: cause me to know the way wherein
I should walk; for I lift up my soul unto Thee.
Deliver me, O Lord, from mine enemies: I flee unto Thee to hide me.
Teach me to do Thy will; for Thou art my God:
Thy spirit is good; lead me into the land of uprightness.
Quicken me, O Lord, for Thy name's sake:
for Thy righteousness' sake bring my soul out of trouble.
And of Thy mercy cut off mine enemies, and destroy all them that
afflict my soul: for I am Thy servant. (Psalm 143:8–12, KJV)*

Peaceful Waters

But whosoever drinketh of the water that I shall give him shall never thirst; but the water that I shall give him shall be in him a well of water springing up into everlasting life. —John 4:14 (KJV)

It is early morn
I sit relaxed before the waters of the bay
In the near distance, a boat peacefully sails the calm waters
and my soul is at ease

My mind turns back for a moment
recalling the times when the waters of my life
were as giant waves
ruthless and all-powerful
ready to engulf me into its mighty arms

I think of the many times I fought against the Master of the Sea
rebelling only against His love
and His perfect will for me
but He has brought me a long ways home
even to this place
as my mind quickly returns to the serenity before me

My heart is grateful for His mercies
and I no longer fight against the currents of His love
for today I accept the place that I must fill
It matters not how great the task before me
Challenges that overwhelmed in the past
are met only by the assurances of His love
the promises of His strength
and the evidences of His power
The place and places I must fill are ordered by the Almighty
in whose wings I have made my hiding place

I leave now this sweet haven of rest
but I take with me the Fountain of Living Waters
that never shall run dry

August 22, 1986

*And the Lord shall guide thee continually, and satisfy thy soul in drought,
and make fat thy bones: and thou shalt be like a watered garden, and
like a spring of water, whose waters fail not. (Isaiah 58:11, KJV)*

Perfect Peace

Thou wilt keep him in perfect peace, whose mind is stayed on Thee: because he trusteth in Thee. —Isaiah 26:3 (KJV)

The heavens are filled with grand display
Of foreboding clouds, dark and gray
The winds blow soft with whisperings
Forcing the trees and bushes to sing
As the lightening streaks across the sky
The thunder resounds an echoed reply
The prelude for the storm is here
Foretelling that the worst is near
And anxious minds run to and fro
What to do?
Where to go?
The turmoil has been born
Even... before the storm

*"O soul of mine remember
God has promised perfect peace"*

The dark clouds roll in as to dominate
And its anger and fury intimidates
The whispering winds now turn severe
Heavy rains, surging waters, arousing fears
The waves go crashing in most fierce
Shooting water arrows meant to pierce
I fear this wrath is aimed at me
The forces of evil have all agreed
On this a cruel conspiracy
To exasperate
To obliterate
The storm is here
And it is great!

"But soul of mine remember
God has promised perfect peace"

We know the certainty of storms
It matters not the shape or form
If Christ Himself is at the helm
What storm can be that overwhelms
The child whose eyes are fixed on Thee
Thou, the *Creator* of the seas
Who ruleth still in dark of night
Behind closed doors my battles fight
And intervenes, else cunning plans
Would place me in the tempter's hands
God overrules so all can see
It is He that confronts this foe—not me

And thus my soul may safely rest
For those beneath His wings are blest
The child "whose mind is stayed on Thee"
Is assured this day of victory
In Christ, we'll ride the wings of storms
Unto His everlasting arms
Though strong and massive *this* storm be
He has promised us *great* peace

O soul embrace and claim it now
What force on earth can disallow
A promise God has given us
If we but place in Him our trust
Holdfast! Our Anchor is secure
The winds will cause our hearts to soar
Above, beyond these furious skies
To the fortress of The Lord Most High

It is there in His most abled hands
He gives us peace that man can't understand
Such amazing love! O how my heart is thrilled
At the One who makes my storms be still!

Indeed, our Father delivers well
For He has rescued my soul from hell
And has claimed me as His own
Never again to walk alone
So I rejoice! I exalt! I lift up His name!
For Jehovah God is still the same
The Beloved, Everlasting, Faithful and Kind
The Prince of Peace
And today, He's mine
Yes, today His peace is mine

"O soul, thou must remember
That though it be a perfect storm
God is our perfect peace"

February 22, 2013

(To my grandson, Joel)

And the peace of God, which passeth all understanding, shall keep your
hearts and minds through Christ Jesus. (Philippians 4:7, KJV)

Great peace have they which love Thy law: and nothing shall offend them. (Psalm 119:165, KJV)

"Return Unto Thy Rest"

Return unto thy rest, O my soul; for the Lord hath dealt bountifully with thee. For Thou hast delivered my soul from death, mine eyes from tears, and my feet from falling. —Psalm 116:7–8 (KJV)

O how cruel and weary this endless night
as I yearn for sleep so desperately
But it seems somehow my anxious mind
has lost its course
Yet above the raging storms
and the cries of violent seas
I hear a still, small voice
that beckons me

"Return unto thy Rest"

Still... the last caress of slumber
slowly fades
for my soul is most disquieted
I am hopelessly distressed
The enemy has his way
for I cannot rest
Even so, with labored breath
and with fierce expectancy
I speak aloud those pressing words

"Return unto thy Rest, O my soul"

I hasten to His throne
and fall on bended knees
before my God
My cries will come before Him
yes, even unto His ears
His clouds, He will make a chariot
and ride in haste to calm my fears

O I can feel Him near
as He attendeth to my tears
and comforts me
And I would stay the whole night through
nearest to His breast
nor ever dare to leave
for here within His arms is peace and rest

"Return unto thy Rest, O my soul"
yes, even unto Christ, your Gracious King

And O how sweet my sleep!
My troubled soul is hushed by His promised perfect peace
for I rest alone in My Beloved
beneath His wings of infinite love
as my Gracious Father spreads His covering over me

O indeed, I have returned
yes, even unto Christ, my Gracious King

January 27, 2013

(To my son, Bryant)

When thou liest down, thou shalt not be afraid: yea, thou shalt lie
down, and thy sleep shall be sweet. (Proverbs 3:24, KJV)

Sweet Meditation

My meditation of Him shall be sweet: I will be glad in the Lord.
—Psalm 104:34 (KJV)

Outside I hear the blowing winds
with its near and distant sounds
and the rhythmic tapping of the rain upon the window pane
incessantly invites me to turn my thoughts aside
and dwell upon the storm that is sure to come
But what can cause my mind to turn from My Beloved
for time with Him is fresh as morning dew
It rejuvenates, invigorates and renews my weary mind
causing my lips to smile
making meditation sweet

Sometimes the mightiest storm in life is not the storm outside
but the storm that beats with cruelty from within
the quickening of the breath
the pounding of the heart
that pit within that slowly turns
and in the belly burns
Anxious mind cannot escape from all that would ensue
until the fearful heart communes my Lord with Thee
And in a moment, in a wink, with all power in Thine hand
Thou doth touch the crippling soul and makes her feet to stand
And how her heart delights in Thee!
And how her tongue gives praise to Thee!
For Thou alone commands her love
and makes meditation sweet

And thus, when darkness turns its ugly head toward me
with seducing eyes determined to ensnare
May to Thy dwelling place I run
yes, to Thy fortress flee

Mine eyes shall look unto Thine hills
with hope's expectancy
and this heart shall whisper in her soul
the one thing that she truly knows:
"There is safety in the One who died for me"
For in the excellence of His greatness
and by the might of His right hand
He shall honor with a great deliverance
'round me angels shall encamp
and my Father, whom I love
will unveil His awesome power
and I shall bask in the gladness of the Lord

Yes, Thou hast made my meditation sweet
because the splendor of Thy love hast captured me
O, Thy great and awesome love hast captured me!

January 31, 2014

(To my goddaughter, Ashly)

The Secret Place

*He that dwelleth in the secret place of the Most High shall abide under
the shadow of the Almighty. —Psalm 91:1 (KJV)*

I have found a secret place
that satisfies the longings of my soul
Here, I am sheltered by a kind and loving Father
The El Shaddai of endless ages is my God
I am safe beneath His massive wings
which are strong and enduring
The storms cannot enter in
My soul dares not venture out
I abide within the inner stillness of my Lord

There is peace here that you cannot fathom
There is rest that soothes the tired and weary soul
He is mine alone
and I am His only
I am abundantly favored by the Sovereign God

Jehovah Jireh—
He *is* my provider
The Strength of Israel, my absolute delight
What joy when I bask in His sweet presence
What warmth that holds me through the coldest night

And I am at home in this quiet place
within the private chambers of my King
And none can enter in without His bidding
Yet, there are some He bids that do not enter in
May I, when maddening throngs would surely have me
make haste Thy blessed, sacred place to dwell
without pause
or the slightest hesitation
but with great anticipation for what awaits

May I abide in Thy dwelling place, O Lord, forever
bound solely unto Thee with chains of love
And with pure heart
lift up my voice in ceaseless praises
unto Thee, the all-consuming lover of my soul

Unto Thee, my Lord
Thou art the sweet lover of my soul

April 15, 2012

(Dedicated to Nicholas Hicks and Nicholas Hicks II)

Thy Fragrance Sweet

For His anger endureth but a moment; in His favour is life: weeping may endure for a night, but joy cometh in the morning. —Psalm 30:5 (KJV)

There are times when at the close of day
When I, distraught, kneel down to pray
I search for worthy words to say
But I find none
I pray my voice would reach Your skies
And hope Your ear will hear my cries
Yet I fall ashamed before Your eyes
For I am undone

I long for strength to do Thy will
So pressing closer to Thee still
I fall prostrate at Calvary's Hill
And call Thy name
For no other name can pierce the night
And charge the enemy swift to flight
And change the course of this sinner's plight
To blessings gained

I seek no help from those around
My eyes are set on higher ground
Unto Thee, my Lord, my soul is bound
I cannot flee
No other counsel than Thine own
No other shelter but Thy throne
There is no help but Thine alone
Please comfort me

Until Thy fragrance sweet I find
Until our hearts are intertwined
Until I feel my hand in Thine
I will not rest
Thou art the Savior of my soul
The only helper that I know
I cling to Thee and won't let go
Till I am blest

So Heavenly Father free me now
As I before Thy presence bow
Release these chains; I know not how
I look to Thee
I have no strength; I have no might
I know that this is not my fight
And so I trust in Thee this night
For victory

Yes, in the morning joy shall come
And I shall find my heart at home
And know that I was not alone
But at Thy feet
For at the dawning of the day
I shall no longer be dismayed
For my soul itself shall be arrayed
In Thy fragrance sweet

Sweet relief from midnight tears
Sweeter peace in surrendered cares
Sweeter still for Thou art here
And mine forevermore!

September 8, 2012

(Dedicated to the loving memory of Mrs. Rose Marie Winfield)

Thy Slumber Shall Be Sweet

When thou liest down, thou shalt not be afraid: yea, thou shalt lie down,
and thy sleep shall be sweet. —Proverbs 3:24 (KJV)

Have you ever had a heavy burden lifted
and in a moment felt the warmth of inner peace
all anxieties, perplexities completely vanished
as if their torment to the soul had never been unleashed
and your deeply laden brow was hushed and comforted
no longer fettered by impending doom
and you wonder, how can one in the midst of mighty storms
have this calm that overturns the wrath of raging seas

It is then that prayer hath proved a mighty fortress
for ofttimes in my bed my thoughts are tossed to and fro
and all the troubles of the day refuse to be assuaged
until I fall on bended knees and cast my cares upon the Lord
and with His gracious hand, He extends the richest blessings
that I of wearied mind hath ever known
for this battle that I fight is not by strength, nor by might
but by the name of God Jehovah to whom I wondrously belong

O Throne of Grace, what a privilege to bow before Thee
to approach The Lord His Majesty and call upon Thy name
and to know that Thou doth bend and tend my cause from Heaven
and hastens to my desperate cries in spite my guilt and shame
O Lamb of God the price You paid for my wandering and erring
hast brought me to Thy nail-scarred feet in gratitude to Thee
I praise Thee for Thy goodness!
I praise Thee for Thy mercy!
and would beg that Thou would make my praise
a dwelling place for Thee!

O I have had a mighty burden lifted
and at this moment know His gift of perfect peace
all anxieties, perplexities completely vanished
as if their torment to my soul had never been unleashed
and my deeply laden brow is now hushed and comforted
no longer fettered by impending doom
and I bear witness there is One in the midst of mighty storms
who has all power to subdue the fury of the raging seas

O I thank You Lord for peace that passeth understanding
that in the midst of vicious storms, it reaches even unto me
Though the turbulence is now raging, and my soul still begs Thy saving
Thou art true to Thy dear promise, Lord; Thou hast made my slumber sweet

April 19, 2019

(To Tasha, with fond memories)

(Dedicated also to First Lady Taunya Grissom, Emmanuel Temple SDA Church)

*And the peace of God, which passeth all understanding, shall keep your
hearts and minds through Christ Jesus. (Philippians 4:7, KJV)*

*I will both lay me down in peace, and sleep: for Thou, Lord,
only makest me dwell in safety. (Psalm 4:8, KJV)*

*It is vain for you to rise up early, to sit up late, to eat the bread of
sorrows: for so He giveth His beloved sleep. (Psalm 127:2, KJV)*

Unto Thee

I carried you on eagles' wings and brought you to Myself.
—Exodus 19:4 (NIV)

Lord, unto Thee...
There is no other place to be
But nearest to the heart of Thine
To cast my soul
For Thou art mine
And though mine eyes no longer see
Beyond this dark that covers me
My hand yet reaches to Thee still
And beg Thy breath my soul to fill
And wait beneath Thy saving cross
Though all seems lost
It shall not be
For Thou hast brought me
Unto Thee

Unto Thee
No sooner there
When I began to lose all cares
Yet higher still on eagles' wings
Unto Thyself my heart doth cling
What love that's marked upon Thy face
Imparting such endearing grace
And joy that cannot be expressed
And peace that brings my soul to rest
The storm that had my heart in tears
Is no longer feared
For Thou art here
Yes, Thou hast drawn me patiently
Firmly, surely
Unto Thee

And when death at last hast taken me
And my latest breath returns to Thee
I shall sleep the slumber of the blest
And in Thee, my Father, I shall rest
Asleep until that glorious day
My eyes awake to see Thy face
My eyes awake to see Thy face!
My King hast come for me to save!
Unspeakable joy! Unutterable bliss!
For He shall be for always mine
and I... forever His

O come Thou quickly Saving Lord
For my soul doth yearn to fly with Thee
Please bear me up on eagles' wings
Unto Thyself, Thy face to see

Yes, unto Thee my Gracious King
For now and all eternity!

October 24, 2012

(Dedicated to the loving memory of my mother-in-law, Sis. Algraphy Graves)

"Why Weepest Thou?"

Jesus saith unto her, "Woman, why weepest thou? whom seekest thou?"
—John 20:15 (KJV)

Why weepest thou, O child of grief
when your Master is standing near
with consolation plentiful
whereby to quiet all your fears
Why aches your heart so heavily
when He Who Saves is by your side
to soothe with heavenly comfort
as beneath His wings you hide
Return to Him, O wandering child
a healing place your soul shall find
Cool waters He will give to you
to refresh your wearied mind
A place of rest is promised you
no need in sorrow's dungeon stay
Arise... and He will show to you
the brilliant light of day!

"Why weepest thou? Whom seeketh thou?"
O how the tears doth blind your eyes
He speaks; yet you cannot discern
the lovely presence of the Risen Christ
awaiting still with outstretched arms
that the weak may be thus fortified
He yearns to give you perfect peace
that faileth not, though fiercely tried
'Tis true, He does *all* things well
and is swift to attend your utmost needs
There is no storm He cannot quell
There is no foe He can't defeat
Yet still you cry as One stands by
who would rescue strong and valiantly

Whom seekest thou? Answer thyself...
It is God for whom you seek

Why weepest thou, O anxious one
when blessed and full can be your days
Upon His bosom, lay now your head
that He may take all fears away
He will give you sight of a better land
that awaits us now with open doors
and there, we'll laugh, we'll sing, we'll dance
and our tears shall be no more

O rejoice my soul! Lift up your head!
Open up your eyes, cast off your cares
for your Lord and Master is not dead
but tarries now to abundantly cheer
O He is alive, forevermore
and your peace and joy He shall restore
O again I ask, how can you weep
when the Lord thy God Almighty...
is here!

March 28, 2021

Have mercy upon me, O Lord, for I am in trouble: mine eye is consumed with grief, yea, my soul and my belly. For my life is spent with grief, and my years with sighing: my strength faileth because of mine iniquity, and my bones are consumed. (Psalm 31:9–10, KJV)

Caring

and

Sharing

The year 2020 was one of the most horrific times in the history of the United States—pandemic deaths, economic devastation, political chaos, systemic racism, social unrest, and moral corruption in high places. These are truly uncertain times, and many are feeling highly stressed, anxious, and, literally, unable to breathe. There is so much suffering and hurt in the world today, and the prospects for the future is indeed hopeless; that is, it would be hopeless if it had not been for Christ. His death at the cross assures us of a bright future where there is no more suffering or death—a place where we shall live peacefully and joyfully together as brothers and sisters in Christ. One day soon, we shall know blessed quietness and uninterrupted calm; for we shall be warmly cradled in the Everlasting arms of our Heavenly Father—and we shall *breathe*! We shall finally... *breathe*!

Beauty of His Face

His mouth is most sweet: yea, He is altogether lovely. This is my Beloved,
and this is my Friend. —Song of Solomon 5:16 (KJV)

How I wish I knew the words that would go straight to your heart
That would tell you of His excellence and the joys His hands impart
Just taste and see and you'll uncover the sweet mysteries of His love
For He is Altogether Lovely... and He is so beautiful!

I have seen the beauty of His face at His birth in Bethlehem
And I heard the angels' voices sing of peace, goodwill toward men
The infant Majesty who saves, O wondrous birth that offers grace
Lo, how the heavenly host bows down as they behold His glorious face

I have seen the beauty of His feet on His walk to Calvary
Nail-scarred and wounded for my sins; what love He's wrought for me
My heart in utmost reverence bows as His selfless steps I trace
And tears shall ever flow unchecked as I gaze upon His face

I have seen the beauty of His hands when He lifted me from night
And raised me ever tenderly to the warmth of His pure light
Even now my heart grows vastly full as His love I contemplate
As I stand in loving, wondrous awe at the splendor of His face

I have seen the beauty of His lips, for His mouth is O most sweet
I've tasted of His graciousness for His voice is life to me
Within my heart I hide His words, treasuring all He would impart
For this *indeed* is my Beloved who hast captured all my heart

And O the beauty of His eyes that searches far and low
Who has held me always in His gaze, just to make His goodness shown
"Keep mine the apple of Thine eye" my heart in whispers say
"May they be ever drawn to Thee and the countenance of Thy face"

O I wish that I could place your hands upon the face of Christ
That you may look into His eyes, if just for a little while
Then you would taste and see and know and beg that you might stay
In the light of His dear presence, beholden to His face

O behold the birth, the life, the death of He who was born to save
The Fairest of Ten Thousands, The High and Lifted Up in Praise
The Everlasting From Everlasting, The Lamb of God that was slain
The King of Kings and The Lord of Hosts! Emmanuel is His name!

August 7, 2015
Revised December 22, 2018

(To my granddaughter, Aryssa)

Blow Upon My Garden

Awake, O north wind; and come, thou south; blow upon my garden, that the spices thereof may flow out. —Song of Solomon 4:16 (KJV)

Lord, "Blow upon my garden"
For there are scents awaiting their release
Sweet fragrances of blessings that hide themselves within
Unseen, until Thy breath exhales the bitter winds
That stirs my soul
And bends me low
Lord, blow upon my garden
That the spices thereof may freely flow

For Thou art my Beloved
And this garden of my heart belongs to Thee
Its tender fruit grows only by Thine hand
Sweet perfumes dispersed at Thine all-wise command
So awake O northern winds; I bid thee come
And blow upon my garden
That the spices of His love may fill the air
Till the sweetness of His breath is everywhere

Lord, it is for Thy praise
That the winds of life ofttimes blow hard and cold
So as to awaken sweet aromas laid to rest
Giving strength to fragrances to dance and laugh
To breathe into the soul who yearns for Thee
To loose the chains of those who would be free
For it is good to taste how gracious Thou art
Thou, the Fair Gardener of my heart
Who hast set mine eyes upon Thine hills
And with Thy plenty I am filled
But they, too, have need to know
So as it pleases Thee, my Lord
Upon my garden blow

Till the balsams of Thy presence fill the air
And the sweetness of Thy love
Is theirs to share

So "awake, O north wind; and come, thou south"
On thy wings, the scent of My Beloved flows out
Yet, if from winds Thou deem that I should rest awhile
Then only breathe upon me, Lord
And they shall taste of Heaven in my smile!

May 24, 2013

(Dedicated to my family)

Encourage Yourself!

And David was greatly distressed; for the people spake of stoning him, because the soul of all the people was grieved, every man for his sons and for his daughters: but David encouraged himself in the Lord his God. —1 Samuel 30:6 (KJV)

Sometimes the battles are overwhelming
And the giants before us are strong
Their armies are massive and unrelenting
And the days and nights grow exhaustingly long
But, it is often the case that some battles we face
Are merely conflicts that are self-imposed—
Hostilities we ordain, doubts we entertain
Which is sometimes to the detriment of our own souls
But God hast offered us *uninterrupted* victories
When to the hills our trusting eyes are set
Therefore, cease the murmuring and wallowing in self-pity
Instead, in the Lord, encourage yourself

There are times when the enemy attacks with ferocity
With intimidating forces, seemingly invincible in might
And the weaponry of war *now* before us is daunting
But we must remember always: This is not our fight
For the awesome God we serve is the Red Sea Divider
He is the God of the fiery furnace and Lord of the lion's den
And the victories that are wrought in impossible situations
Are never won in the strength and might of mortal men
But what we need today are Davids, Joshuas and Calebs
Who would rally us *forthwith* into God's armory of defense
Be not dismayed, be not disheartened, be not disillusioned
But be ye admonished... encourage yourself!

Hast God ever forsaken us in trouble?
Hast He not been a "present help" and constant friend?

We should recall the evidences of His love and favor
And not be overtaken by discouragement and discontent
For the Lord God Almighty *is* mighty
The whole of His creation bows down at His command
And He will deliver us out of this wilderness experience
And restore an everlasting possession of Canaan's Land
But if your soul hast lost its courage and is drowning in unbelief
And your once-hopeful spirit is left wanting and bereft
Then break down those prison walls of fear and trepidation
And in the Lord God Jehovah, encourage yourself

"For God hath not given us the spirit of fear
But of power, and of love, and of a sound mind"
And hast promised to be gracious, never leave nor forsake us
And His promises are especially empowered for these times
So let us look to the Lord for *His* counsel and wisdom
And lean not to our own understanding
For our thoughts are not His thoughts; our ways are not His ways
And our arms are not the arms of the Ever Strong and Everlasting

Yes, challenging are the times that lie ahead of us
But so much greater is the God that resides in us
Hold foremost in your memories the precious testimonies of His love
And encourage yourself *continually...* in the Lord!

February 23, 2021

For God hath not given us the spirit of fear; but of power, and
of love, and of a sound mind. (2 Timothy 1:7, KJV)

For My thoughts are not your thoughts, neither are your ways My ways, saith
the Lord. For as the heavens are higher than the Earth, so are My ways higher
than your ways, and My thoughts than your thoughts. (Isaiah 55:8–9, KJV)

God Has Forgiven Me

*And be ye kind one to another, tenderhearted, forgiving one another,
even as God for Christ's sake hath forgiven you. —Ephesians 4:32 (KJV)*

God has forgiven me
Though my sins were as angry seas
Deep, wide, crashing waves
With fluid hands that cannot save
And lost at sea, this was my lot
Until the day I found my God
He wore compassion in His eyes
With hands that beckoned me to rise
It was He that came and searched for me
Though hell was sure my destiny
And it mattered not how low my state
I asked forgiveness... and He forgave

But if I were God, I wonder then
If I would so easily forgive the sins
Of those who brought me grief and pain
And caused my heart to bend in shame
Would I forgive the hand that strikes
The abuser that works his deeds in the night
The haters who twisted the truth with their lies
With piercing, cruel words that made me cry
Or the killers who have taken our children away
And those who left scars that remain to this day
The friends that betrayed and mocked at my trust
The mean and the ugly, the unkind and unjust

God has forgiven all of such things
And yet to our grudges and dislikes we cling
Our petty emotions we let rule our lives
Our disdain, our distaste, our conflicts and strife

God forgives much, so who are we
To hoard our forgiveness when He forgiveth all things
Thank God He is The God who is worthy of all praise
He yet searches for us though we've turned from His ways
He is loving and faithful, not like man at all
Always there to forgive us when we stumble and fall

Loving Father, please teach us to forgive and forget
And when it seems too hard to just "let go of it"
Remind us the enemy's heart is made glad
When we hold on to bitterness, anger and wrath
For the rehearsing of injuries that has wounded our souls
Will keep us in darkness with no place to go
Unforgiveness is a chain that binds up our hearts
And holds us as prisoners in cells of the dark
Forgive to be forgiven: this mandate is Thine
Thus we pray for Your power to forgive that's divine
Impart Your sweet Spirit; set us on a true course
Showing mercy for others; none are of less worth
And when conflicts arise, may we then honor Thee
With the words "I forgive you, for God has forgiven me!"

April 7, 2012

(To my granddaughter, Jasmyn)

And forgive us our debts, as we forgive our debtors. (Matthew 6:12, KJV)

His Shadow

Because Thou hast been my help, therefore in the shadow of Thy wings will I rejoice. —Psalm 63:7 (KJV)

Keep me as the apple of the eye, hide me under the shadow of Thy wings. —Psalm 17:8 (KJV)

As I journey back reluctantly in years of time gone by
I observe the shattered life of a helpless, broken child
I feel her loss of innocence; I share her fear of night
Yet my grasp for understanding is far from realized

There amongst the tangled briers and sharply thorns
Lies scattered, fragile fragments of childhood dreams unborn
And with resounding voice I hear the screams of silent tears
Which belies the ever-presence of One who lingers near

What to do when a heart is left destitute, alone?
Where to go when what lies ahead is daunting and unknown?
For the enemy is real, his weapons fierce and strong
And a timid child lies powerless before his mighty throng

Yet, behind the evil dealings of all unjustly kings
Behind their ugly secrets and their shrewd maneuverings
There remains a shadow strong of which I can't deny
A quiet, constant presence that extends beyond my eyes

Such painful, haunting memories of despairing, hopeless days
Make me fall abruptly to my knees, consumed, but cannot pray
For my anguished heart is troubled; it is night and I'm afraid
I wonder what has brought me back to this most dreadful place

And suddenly as I fight in vain against black rememberings
I feel my Father's presence, so warm and comforting
The shadow of His presence, unperceived in my dark past
And with gifted new awareness, I understand at last

It was my Heavenly Father who kept me through those years
Unbeknownst to His dear promise, He was always there
For when the mighty held me fast with grossly weighted chains
He would spread His wings above me; somehow I was sustained

My Father knew one day that I would take His saving hands
And waited patiently beside me in spite of lesser plans
To think the hovering winds of strife His hands held back for me
I am humbled by the thought; today where would I be?

I am blest His eyes were on me when His love I did not know
That in the dark of fearful night, He sought to save my soul
And I have come to know for certain of this one glorious thing:
I was kept beneath the shadow of God's almighty wings

And still today the enemy lies crouching and in wait
To pounce upon the child of God who would walk the narrow way
His eyes are keen as he seeks his prey; I'm no match for his dark schemes
So Father, cover me with Thy feathers; hide me safe beneath Thy wings

And may those I meet who have fallen prey beneath a predator's hand
May I lift Thee up so Thou may draw their minds to understand
That it matters not how deep one falls into the depths of hell
We have a Blessed, Saving Christ who maketh all things well

And thus, I leave my past behind and press forward toward the mark
Forever grateful Thou hast brought me nearest to Thine heart
The sweetest psalms of highest praise forever I shall sing
For now I live unto Thee, Father, beneath the shadow of Thy wings

Yes, He, whom my soul loves greatly, in whom my heart delights
Now holds me safe within His arms
And I no longer fear the night!
I no longer *fear* the night!

August 15, 2013

(Dedicated to my sisters, Delores & Rose Mary)

But this one thing I do, forgetting those things which are behind, and reaching forth unto those things which are before, I press toward the mark for the prize of the high calling of God in Christ Jesus. (Philippians 3:13–14, KJV)

"Let the Redeemed of the Lord Say So"

Let the redeemed of the Lord say so, whom He hath redeemed from the hand of the enemy. —Psalm 107:2 (KJV)

I see the faces of those who show no honor to Thy name
Who cannot fully understand the language of my praise
Hearts bent and torn and lost, eyes emptied and unknowing
And I ache that they would somehow feel the wonders of Thy grace
My grateful heart gives sudden pause at the praise that I would share
For it seems all too apparent, this is not what they would hear
It is then I realize that it is I who stand alone
In a strange and distant land far from home
Missing so the kindred voices of those who hold Thee dear
Longing for the ole familiar, wishing I was somehow there
Wondering how a child of God can voice Thy praise in desolation
Where waxen hearts deny the precious gift of Thy salvation

But then I get a glimpse of Heaven and the saints who will gather there
I stand in awe at Thy glorious face, forgetting every earthly care
I see Thine hand reach out to mine, and I touch the nail scars of Thy love
And fall unworthy at Thy feet, overwhelmed, but yet so full
For all around I hear the voices of the redeemed from age to age
I can feel the beat of each grateful heart; O I understand their praise
For they attest of Thy goodness and mercies and the great debt of love they owe
And their resounding hallelujahs touch a chord in my own soul
O what wondrous joy to be finally home in the presence of my Lord
But then suddenly the vision fades, and I'm returned to this ole earth

But return I must for there are souls who are lost outside the fold
And the praises of Heaven still urges me on: O "let the Redeemed of the Lord say so!"
If God hath rescued thee from night and out of the hand of thine enemy
Will thy voice be hushed in silence when the Most High God hath delivered thee?
Then let us speak of His goodness and mercies, even to hearts who don't believe
To the downcast and the weary, to the rebellious, the broken, the weak
Though praise may fall on hardened ears, it is the Spirit who quickens and revives
From the deep dark depths of the enemy's grasp to the light of the heavenly skies

O let all that is *in* you bless Him; bless the Lord, O my soul!
If God hath raised *you* up from death, then let the risen of the Lord say so
One day soon we shall receive an inheritance that is eternal, incorruptible, undefiled
We'll greet the once-dimmed faces of the downcast, whom to the Father are now reconciled
And the Light of our lives shall dwell among us, The Lamb of God, the Savior our King
His kingdom shall reign everlasting, as well as the melodious praises of the redeemed
O let the purchased of the Lord say so—He who has been ransomed by the Great I Am
For indeed, this soul has been redeemed! I've been redeemed out of the enemy's hand!

I've been redeemed by the blood of the Lamb!

June 11, 2017

Live Inside of Me

For to me to live is Christ, and to die is gain.—Philippians 1:21 (KJV)

A Covid-19 Pandemic Prayer

What a strange new world before us, Lord
the likes of which hast not been known—
Evil thrives on fertile ground
and it grows and grows and grows
Men's hearts are in such dire distress
as we live our daily lives apart
from loved ones that are near to us—
as though they were afar
So live inside of me, my Lord
that I may be Your weathered feet
to cross the path of the suffering
who walks unaware of Thee
Guide my steps that I might serve
Thy beckoned call, compassionately
Live inside of me, my Lord
that I may live for Thee

Fear is rampant all around
as we face the great unknown
It seems throughout Earth's vast expanse
We are all in this together—yet alone
And thus we yearn for loving arms
an embrace, a touch, a kiss
in lieu of on-screen images
replacing bustling lives once lived
So dwell inside of me, my Lord
that I may be Your gracious hands
to hold the frames of loneliness
of the grieving, the dying friend

Reach beyond the stark confines
of this lowly, mortal being
and live Thy life inside of me
that I may love for Thee

And when I'm sorely overwhelmed
by this world's dark atrocities
staggering beneath its heaviness
may I upon Thy bosom lean
reassured Thou art the King of Kings
on whom my wretched soul depends
Remind me sweetly once again
of how this story ends...
In the presence of Thy glory
I then shall see Thee face to face
and be known of Thee for eternity
in the warmth of Thine embrace
as the redeemed from age to age
bestows abundant praise to Thee
on account of Thy great sacrifice
expressly shown at Calvary
Thus, Lord, I entreat of Thee...

Make my heart Thy habitation
May Thine Holy Spirit sweep o'er my life
that I may walk in full with Thee
For to me... to live is Christ!

May 13, 2020

(Dedicated to a special daughter, Evelyne Luka)

I am crucified with Christ: nevertheless I live; yet not I, but Christ liveth in me: and the life which I now live in the flesh I live by the faith of the Son of God, who loved me, and gave Himself for me. (Galatians 2:20, KJV)

Mary's Little Lamb

Whoso offereth praise glorifieth Me: and to him that ordereth his conversation aright will I shew the salvation of God. —Psalm 50:23 (KJV)

She was magnificent!
Her words were clear, precise and articulate
Her message was timely, significant and legitimate
And I, impressed with her command of the profession
stood in awe of her poetic expression
yet suddenly felt inadequate, inferior
for in spite of her youthful exterior
she was perfectly poised and seemingly superior
and most certainly destined for notoriety and fame
and I?—well I felt somewhat ashamed
as I thought on the verses I hitherto wrote
which now seems in likeness to—and I quote:
"Mary had a little lamb
its fleece was white as snow"
yes, a child's simple nursery rhyme
written long ago

Well, my Father above, who is ever gracious
who has covered me with love, and yes, with much patience
bent His ear to my pitiful sigh
shook His head and whispered, "My child"
then He hastened at once to my side
spoke these words as He looked in my eyes

"But child... Mary did have a little lamb
and that little lamb was Me
I am the perfect sacrifice
The Lamb of God who died for Thee
And when someone speaks my name
walks in My ways, gives Me the praise
whether it be in some simple verse
or grand, prolific and majestic words

or spoken in the presence of the great of the Earth
or heard in the company of commoners—
that righteous praise breaks wide
the infinite barriers of space and time
and enters into My dwelling place
and is set before My face
and I, The Lord Thy Savior, doth *all* gratefulness embrace
Yes, Mary had a little lamb; this verse seems but a little thing
but I, the Worthy Lamb of God, am Lord of Lords and King of Kings—
I am He of whom the herald angels sang!
O child, it matters not how humble or simple the words
all praise is heard
for all praise belongs to Me"

Well... I was quite humbled by my Father's kindly reprimand
but I was also delighted as to how hugely blessed I am
that the Majesty of Heaven stepped down from His throne above
uplifted my failing spirit, as He instructed me in love
My foolish thoughts, He checked
My soul, He then refreshed
What kind of God would do that for me!
What kind of God takes note of me?
and swift to my side intercepts
to lovingly guard my steps

O God's love is truly Transcendent!
It surpasses all that is beautiful and resplendent
It intervenes, intercedes, supersedes and provides...
to the wanting, abundant riches
to the dying, abundant life
The depraved, and the degenerate
are made virtuous and most reverent
and a sinner, such as me
is made free

O I am grateful for the cross that was raised
and shall lavish Him for always with praise
Though our words may be simple, moderate or grand
they shall permeate the ears of Mary's Little Lamb
and resonate through the vastness of all eternity
for *all* praises, O Lord, belong to Thee!

And oh, by the way, just so you know...
His fleece was actually *whiter* than snow!

February 14, 2021

(Dedicated to Mimi's little lambs: Silas, Dexter & Jocelynn, Mariella & Zane, Jadyn & Kai)

Behold the Lamb of God, which taketh away the sin of the world. (John 1:29, KJV)

To the end that my glory may sing praise to Thee, and not be silent. O Lord my God, I will give thanks unto Thee for ever. (Psalm 30:12, KJV)

Sweet Exchange

I am come that they might have life, and that they might have it more abundantly. —John 10:10 (KJV)

Sometimes our present needs can seem quite overwhelming
When we would think about the tasks that lie ahead
And the mind gets clogged and wearied with limited resources
While demands are towering steadily above our heads
And we would faint beneath the cloud sorely pressed upon us
And with each sigh, our woeful soul cries greatly for release
But O to know that I have found a kind and wondrous Savior
Who would exchange my anxious fears for His own peace

There are times when trials of life seem constant, never-ending
When one deeply darkened cloud has passed, then another quickly forms
And O the wrath in which the foe pursues his would-be captives
It is his hope that we would finally break beneath the storm
But I have found that in each storm there lies the richest blessings
I have truly learned from the bitterest grief, there is yet delight
For I have found a merciful and gracious loving Savior
Who would exchange my dreaded darkness for His pure light

And because of this, my heart knows peace from God's enduring presence
Which often makes my eyes swell up with profoundly grateful tears
When I consider that I am indeed a child of His own glory
And all Heaven's riches belong to me and are ever near
O I can feel the holy breaths of His angelic host about me
I can faintly hear the wafting of their mighty stalwart wings
For they are sent upon request from the "Altogether Lovely"
The Most High God, Jehovah, my Beloved King

If you one day should find yourself in the midst of darkest night
And your trembling heart lies fearful beneath black and heavy clouds
And you feel that all have left you to struggle on your own
And you know that of yourself, there is surely no way out

Then, my child, you must at once look up and remember Grammie's Jesus
And recall some words of joyful praise He poured into her heart
He will exchange your heavy burdens with all its dark forebodings
For His abundant life and the purest, richest blessings it imparts

One day soon night shall leave us, and it shall not return again
In just a little while, we will walk through Heaven's door
We'll spend eternity in adoration of the dear Christ of our salvation
Forever His! Forever ours! Thus it shall be forevermore!
But as for now, it is my prayer that you will give your heart to Jesus
For His kind and abled hands will more than supply your every need
Now is the time to know Him; O He will make your heart to love Him!
My Sweet Jesus... is awaiting now to give you peace

April 26, 2015

(To my children, grandchildren and great-grandchildren)

Come unto Me, all ye that labour and are heavy laden, and I will give you rest. Take My yoke upon you, and learn of Me; for I am meek and lowly in heart: and ye shall find rest unto your souls. For My yoke is easy, and My burden is light. (Matthew 11:28–30, KJV)

Sweet Freedom!

*Stand fast therefore in the liberty wherewith Christ hath made us free,
and be not entangled again with the yoke of bondage.*
—Galatians 5:1 (KJV)

If the Son therefore shall make you free, ye shall be free indeed.
—John 8:36 (KJV)

O Thou, Lord, who upholds the heavens and Earth
and art privy still to our wayfaring cries
The most secret of places are known to Thee
There is nothing that escapes Thine eyes
Even now in the deep and dark confines
of the enemy's horrendous and powerful grasp
we are enslaved, Lord; we are held as prisoners
to the sins that so easily besets
for we find ourselves in faraway places
shackled and bound in *unbreakable* bands
forgetting that the God whose dwellings are afar
is a *God who saves...* and is close at hand

With failing sight, Lord, and with deafly ears
we no longer see the brilliance of Thy face
Thy voice is but a low and distant murmur
that hast lost its savor, form and shape
for Thy children, Lord, are in captivity
We have rejected Thy covenant to bless
but with outstretched arms, O Thou art pleading still
that we may return unto Thy Bosom of Rest
And we who spurn Thy tender loving pleas
seek after idols of nefarious sorts
not knowing that the God who is close at hand
pronounces judgements from on high in Heaven's courts

And thus, O Gracious Father, we entreat of Thee
return us swiftly unto Thy refuge of safety
Breathe in us new life; make us free in Christ
that we no more may be entangled in slavery
For Jesus broke asunder the chains of bondage
that in the here-and-now, we may walk in liberty
For He, who is the sinner's Emancipator
is also He, who inhabits Eternity!

Hence... freedom has a name—O it is Jesus!
Freedom has a name—Jesus Christ!
The dear and precious Lamb of Calvary
The Marvelous, The Wonderful, The Supreme Sacrifice
O we give Thee, Lord, the highest praise, for we *have* been redeemed
for Thou hast heard our desperate cries and hath delivered from afar
Though Thou hast set Thy lovely dwellings in a high and holy place
Thou hast made Thy earthly residence in the humble, contrite heart

Yes, freedom has a name—it is Jesus
(for if the Son hath made you free
then you are free indeed!)
O let us bless the name of Jesus—for He is Freedom!
He is Freedom, O Sweet Freedom over me!

June 17, 2021

For thus saith the high and lofty One that inhabiteth eternity, whose
name is Holy; I dwell in the high and holy place, with him also that
is of a contrite and humble spirit. (Isaiah 57:15, KJV)

Am I a God at hand, saith the Lord, and not a God afar off? Can any
hide himself in secret places that I shall not see him? saith the Lord.
Do not I fill Heaven and Earth? (Jeremiah 23:23-24, KJV)

Thou Art God!

For Thou art great, and doest wondrous things: Thou art God alone.
—Psalm 86:10 (KJV)

Lately I've been musing about the darker side
the cares, the fears
the loss of love and life
hunger, hatred, cruelty and abuse
powers misaligned, misapplied and woefully misused
lies, fabrications, misinformation, manipulation
extreme conspiracies and runaway imaginations
sicknesses, diseases with restorative delays
not knowing what tomorrow holds
but knowing fear will yet pervade
What is this helplessness, this hopelessness
this meaningless demise?
And what of these sudden outbursts
of tears and sighs?

But lest we forget...
"God so loved the world that He gave"
with the blood of His own Son, my life to save
O Thou most beautiful and perfect sacrifice
source of strength, springs of hope, joy of life
Thou makes meaningful the utter meaningless
Thou art the healer of all diseases and illnesses
Thou breaks asunder prison walls of animosity
delivering high and mightily from sin's monstrosities
Thou forgiveth our trespasses and iniquities
crowning us with kindnesses and tender mercies
Thou art yet the great divider of formidable seas
felling giants who rule corrupt and pretentiously
For Thou art God who cradles still the whole world in Thine hands
Thou Blessed Christ, the Son of God and, too, the Son of Man

Thou giveth Living Waters, Lord, to all who are athirst
Bread of Life to the hungered, blessings to those accursed
Seeker of my heart, though I am foolish, wretched, blind
gifted fully unto me, yet betrothed to all mankind
Unto the wandering perisher, Thou art life; Thou art breath
Valiant Guardian of the grave, Mighty Conqueror of death
For Thou art God; and ruleth still with preeminent control
Thou art God; and even more, the Savior of my soul

One day soon—yes very soon—Thy glorious face we shall see
We shall soar with wings as eagles and fly home to be with Thee
We shall walk on streets of gold upon entering into Thy gates
We shall know no more wars, no more pain, no more hate
We shall praise Thee with our voices, dances, instruments and songs
sweet expressions of great affection unto Him who grace the Throne
Because Thy love hath known no boundaries, our gratitude will know no end
and throughout the ages of Glory, Thou shalt be loved over and over again
Yes, unto Thee, Thou Blessed Redeemer, for every battle Thou hast won
we bow in deference before Thy presence... for Thou art God alone!

Lord, we adore Thee! We salute Thee! We bless and exalt Thee!
for today, our wearied steps Thou doth graciously regard
Thou giveth hope! *Thou* giveth help! *Thou* giveth strength! *Thou* giveth life!
for Thou—all by Thyself—art God!

February 12, 2021

*For God so loved the world that He gave His only begotten Son, that whosoever
believeth in Him should not perish, but have everlasting life. (John 3:16, KJV)*

Thou art my God, and I will praise Thee: Thou art my God, I will exalt Thee. (Psalm 118:28, KJV)

*Bless the Lord, O my soul, and forget not all His benefits: Who forgiveth all thine
iniquities; who healeth all thy diseases; Who redeemeth thy life from destruction; who
crowneth thee with lovingkindness and tender mercies. (Psalm 103:2–4, KJV)*

We Shall Breathe!

Blessed are the peacemakers: for they shall be called the children of God.
—Matthew 5:9 (KJV)

Unrest, oppressed, civil disobedience
unrighteous indignation
words—shallow, therefore meaningless
despair, unfair, racial inequality
disheartened and downtrodden
I cannot breathe; I cannot breathe

Social injustice and all-divisive rhetoric
high places corrupt and increasingly degenerate
Does a Black life matter
and, too, the taking of the knee
as the world looks on in disbelief
upon those who utter, "I cannot breathe"

Systemic racism, demoralized brutality
monuments and symbols of hatred and hostility
lies, deceit and shameful dark atrocities
I cannot breathe! I cannot breathe!
I cannot hold these tears in me!
They must be felt; they must be seen
because I, too, have a dream

O search your heart intently amid this cruel and suffering world
Find your voice—it matters, and refuse to be unheard
Be the change you seek; and one day soon, we will be free
in the peace and calm of Everlasting arms—we shall breathe!

We shall finally... breathe!

June 13, 2020

He hath shewed thee, O man, what is good; and what doth
the Lord require of thee, but to do justly, and to love mercy,
and to walk humbly with thy God? (Micah 6:8, KJV)

Winter Blessings

But He knoweth the way that I take: when He hath tried me, I shall come forth as gold. —Job 23:10 (KJV)

Come see the tall beech tree outside my window
standing barren and alone amid the drifting snow
its weathered branches reaching ever upward
as if seeking refuge from the bitter cold
And within my heart, a kindred bond awakens
for I weary, too, of winter and all it has in store
and wonder deep within my soul, "Why must we suffer
the cruel attacks of dark and dismal storms?"

Then there before my eyes I see a panoramic view
of thunder, lightning, winds and rains
from a frigid winter past
where the enemy of my wretched soul
holds me firmly in his deadly grasp
and demands my fall that I may rise no more

My breath is dry and labored
and the beating of my anxious heart
is pounding hard for eager, itching ears to hear
What is this desolation?
Why such dreadful trepidation?
Who is this nameless, faceless, mighty enemy I fear?

This truly is a storm
a grand and massive storm
the greatest of the battles to be fought
And I would surely faint beneath this overwhelming load
that is—I would have fainted, *if it had not been for God!*

My every limb and branch looks upward
to the Bright and Morning Star
and my soul doth humbly beg
the Sweet Balm of Gilead
to come down again and heal my wounded heart
For He who knows the pathways of a hundred billion stars
knows, too, the way I take, and will release me from these bars
Is there anything too hard for *God*?
Is there *anything* too hard for God?
No indeed! There is not a foe that is greater, Lord, than Thee!

Come see the tall beech tree outside my window
standing stately and majestically alone
with its diamond-covered branches, uplifted to the heavens
soaring high above the white and glistening snow
Today, I see the splendor of its beauty
Today, I know the secret of its everlasting arms
For in God, herein doth lie the most beautiful of winter
for He holds the unseen blessings
found in each and every storm

God is the Hidden Treasure of the storm!

January 30, 2019

(Dedicated to Gregory McCreary)

*Behold, I am the Lord, the God of all flesh: is there any
thing too hard for Me? (Jeremiah 32:27, KJV)*

Family

and

Friends

Separation from family and friends is one of the many tragedies of the Covid-19 pandemic. Social distancing, although necessary, has robbed us of one of our most basic needs—the human touch. If anything good has come out of this horrific pandemic, it would be the acute realization of this incredible blessing that family and friends bring to our lives. At the time of this writing, my heart is still aching for the hugs and kisses of my loved ones, and I am greatly anticipating that special moment when I can give each of them that first *huge, forever* hug. But most importantly, I am especially looking forward to the day when I finally shall see my Beloved Jesus face-to-face. O what a day that will be! And even more, I will be able to embrace Him with a *huge*, *forever* hug again and again and again— yes, throughout the full expanse of all eternity! O be assured my family, be thus assured my friends; we shall never, never part again!

God Knows

*But unto you that fear My name shall the Sun of Righteousness arise
with healing in His wings. —Malachi 4:2 (KJV)*

What other hand, but Thine
can heal the wounded soul
and strengthen he who trusts in Thee
though in misery his grievance soars
though none can hear or feel the pain
God knows
and unto those that fear His name
"shall the Sun of Righteousness arise
with healing in His wings"

Thy languisher entreats, implores
to Thou who makes the broken whole
as the stricken body waxes sore
so too the pondering of the soul
is there no balm in Gilead?
is there no watch upon this bed?
make haste O Master Healer
make haste and comfort now
for Thou alone can soothe and smooth
the wearied, bended brow

As days and nights evolve as one
and the hands of time creep slowly by
the hour of healing has come and gone
but, alas, not so the piercing sighs
where is Thy restoration Lord?
must one thus fall to rise no more?
it seems I pray in vain
yet trust in Thee alone remains
for all that matters is...
God knows
and in His time shall rise again

Whether it be disease or ills
or the woes of a sin-sick life
with healing in His glorious wings
the Sun of Righteousness shall rise
and will teach us songs in the midst of night
sweet songs not learned by morning light
and He who has allowed this pain
will give sure cause to smile again

O be assured, my love, God knows
He knows the way you take
your health and strength He shall restore
and will raise you up to a better day
and in the fullness of His time
when Michael stands in grand array
He too shall raise you one last time
but this time—
it will be to a better place

O yes indeed, my love
ours will be a *better* place!

June 10, 2019

(Dedicated to my loving husband, Benjamin)

But He knoweth the way that I take: when He hath tried me,
I shall come forth as gold. (Job 23:10, KJV)

Is there no balm in Gilead; is there no physician there? why then is not the
health of the daughter of my people recovered? (Jeremiah 8:22, KJV)

Then shall thy light break forth as the morning, and thine health shall
spring forth speedily: and thy righteousness shall go before thee; the
glory of the Lord shall be thy rereward. (Isaiah 58:8, KJV)

Great-Grandparents' Anniversary

Now also when I am old and grayheaded, O God, forsake me not; until I have shewed Thy strength unto this generation, and Thy power to every one that is to come. —Psalm 71:18 (KJV)

Great-Grandma Graves and Pops
We really love you lots!
For you took us in your hearts
Right from the very start
From Easter eggs to birthday cards
And bags of goodies too
You take the time to share your love
In everything you do

Whenever we come to visit you
Your love is always shown
You talk with us; you laugh with us
You say, "Oh, how you've grown!"
You take the time to listen
To our chatter and our songs
And it never seems to bore you
When Brittany goes on and on

Today we give our thanks to God
He's blessed us through your love
Your prayers have touched upon our lives
With blessings from above
"Oh yes, Jesus, love me"
We know this must be true
Because our Heavenly Father
Gave us the sweetest gift in you

We're blessed indeed to have you
In our growing family
You're the reason we are here today
For without you, we wouldn't be
So to our Great-Grandparents
Who are our dearest gift
We congratulate the both of you
On an awesome sixty-fifth!

Happy Anniversary!
Love, Brittany, Joel, Jasmyn and Aryssa

May 28, 2005

*(Written for Algraphy and Hugh Graves for their 65th Anniversary Celebration
on behalf of their great-grandchildren)*

Greatest Friend

Ointment and perfume rejoice the heart: so doth the sweetness of a man's friend by hearty counsel. —Proverbs 27:9 (KJV)

Dear friend, you're sent from God
To travel with me for a while
For He in His infinite wisdom
Knew I would need a smile
He knew one day I would stumble
So He hastened to my defense
And out of the depths of His goodness
He sent the heavenly gift of a friend

Yes friend, you're sent from God
In answer to my prayers
And oh what comfort sweet it is
To know that someone truly cares
To know someone believes in you
In light of day or deep of night
To know that someone loves you still
Whether you're wrong or right

A wonderful blessing indeed you are
God knew I needed to share
The joys He sends to me each day
The strength of two in prayer
And just in case I fall astray
Afar from His guiding hand
He sends me one who lifts me up
Yes, the beautiful gift of a friend

My friend, you're sent from God
And truly grateful I shall ever be
For just as He has gifted you
He is also gifting me

I too will share His wondrous love
O Christ, the Sacrificial Lamb
Who gave the world His all in all
To become man's Greatest Friend

June 22, 1979

*Greater love hath no man than this, that a man lay down
his life for his friends. (John 15:13, KJV)*

*Henceforth I call you not servants; for the servant knoweth not what his
lord doeth: but I have called you friends; for all things that I have heard
of My Father I have made known unto you. (John 15:15, KJV)*

Handkerchief of Tears

I am troubled; I am bowed down greatly; I go mourning all the day long.
—Psalm 38:6 (KJV)

In loving memory of my father, Earl Riley (January 18, 1935–October 9, 1992)

As I walk into this lonely room
This room of sad goodbyes
And I see you sleeping peacefully
My soul begins to cry
I weep for all those years gone by
Of shattered hopes and dreams
I weep for that which could have been
That now can never be

Hello, Father, it's been so long
Since I've looked upon your face
And strange it is that I still long
For your loving warm embrace
The many years that passed up by
Our separate lives, our separate worlds
Forgetting this—I come today
As Daddy's little girl

It seems those here that knew you best
Can hold within their memories
Sweet recollections of the past
That's been denied to me
And as my eyes with envy gaze
Upon their grieving frames
A strange resentment fills my heart
For this is their loss, their pain

And yet they too will never know
Just what you were to me
Existing always in my heart
Where none but God could see
A heart filled with unspoken words
That should have long been told
We missed the chance that would have turned
Our heartstrings into gold!

For all I have for you just now
Is a handkerchief of tears
No cries for just this weary day
But for all those silent years
My heart bends low with deep lament
Such as I've never known
Regretful grief, it binds me!
Now that our chance is gone

Hello, Father, hello
We meet, and now we part
I leave you sleeping peacefully
I'll awake you in my heart
Hello, Daddy, I love you still
I loved you all the while
We've always wanted to say "hello"
But never, never...

Goodbye

January 22, 1993

I Thought of You Today

The Lord watch between me and thee, when we are absent one from another. —Genesis 31:49 (KJV)

I thought of you today
Just for a little while
And sweetly basked in the memories
Of unforgotten smiles
With pure and sheer delight
We spoke of Jesus' love
And made plans to meet again one day
In His heavenly courts above

You jogged with me today
And how I loved it so
The thoughts we shared together
Are more precious than you know
We made brand new discoveries
In things we both had felt
Again we saw the love of God
In a simple little seashell

You cried with me today
Over a love now gone
My heart was terribly wounded
I felt so all alone
But beyond the tears I saw
My Heavenly Father's care
Divine strength I had found
As we met our Jesus there

And now we softly smile
At the closing of the day
Again we walk those same of old streets
And before we part our ways

We lift our thoughts heavenward
Alone, just you and I
You prayed with me tonight, dear friend
Beneath the starry skies

June 21, 1979

(To my college friend, Angela Boudreaux)

Joyful Celebration!

For yet a little while, and He that shall come will come, and will not tarry.
—Hebrews 10:37 (KJV)

In a moment, in the twinkling of an eye, at the last trump: for the trumpet shall sound, and the dead shall be raised incorruptible, and we shall be changed. So when this corruptible shall have put on incorruption, and this mortal shall have put on immortality, then shall be brought to pass the saying that is written, Death is swallowed up in victory. O death, where is thy sting? O grave, where is thy victory?
—1 Corinthians 15:52, 54-55 (KJV)

In just a little while there shall be a climatic culmination
When the clouds shall suddenly part in a thunderous declaration
And "He that shall come, will come" in splendorous illumination
To take His children home with Him to a most glorious destination
We shall journey among the stars of the heavenly constellations
Our hearts and minds shall be brightly filled with celestial observations
Where all around is pure wonderment and eager anticipation
For the home our Father has prepared for us; O it will surpass the imagination

Gone forever is all sorrow and woeful lamentations
Gone too the curse of death and its painful separations
For "we shall be changed" and lifted up to an everlasting habitation
To dwell no more in the blackened throes of sin and degradation
Yes, soon our eyes shall behold the Sweet Lamb of our Affection
"In the twinkling of an eye" the slumbering shall know of resurrection
This mortal shall put on immortality and death shall cease its domination
And we shall abide in majestic beauty with the most stupendous accommodations

O Family, don't you get weary with Earth's sorrows, trials and tribulations
Don't you long to be in a perfect place that is built on a Sure Foundation
You see, this world is not our home; Earth holds no fascinations
Her streets are dark and the inhabitants know not that they live in desolation

But to spend eternity with Jesus—this is our highest aspiration
For His precious blood delivers us now from the pit of hell's damnation
So it's hard to imagine not being there at His Majesty's royal coronation
In the presence of He who is worthy indeed of all praise and admiration

One day soon we shall cast down our crowns at His feet in adoration
Hallelujahs and hosannas we shall shout with resounding acclamation
Our Blessed Hope is consummate; it has met its realization
The Almighty God triumphant stands before unfallen worlds and nations
O lift up your heads, all ye saints! Lift up in praise and exaltations!
Behold the King of Glory! The Most Beloved of all generations!
His righteous life has covered us; His death, the supreme oblation
Who Was, and Is and Forever Shall Be, the Sweet Lamb of our Salvation

And so, my Family, I now submit to you for your careful consideration:
Are we ready for home in glory? Are we eagerly making preparations?
Are we earnestly striving and advancing by faith to the heights of Christian perfection?
And sharing with others the gift of God's love and the price that was paid for redemption
For we are, by adoption, the children of God, a royal priesthood, a holy nation
And should show forth all praises to Him in our hearts, in our lives and all conversations

O Family of God, don't you long to behold Him in that day of His glorious visitation
When He returns to Earth's skies and we ascend unto Him in an eternal reconciliation
Today, hear His voice as he extends once again this most generous and gracious invitation:
"Come... dine with *Me* My children." Indeed, this shall be the most joyful of celebrations!

September 30, 2015
Revised December 14, 2019

(Dedicated to the loving memory of Mother Ruth Davis)

Little Sister

O taste and see that the Lord is good: blessed is the man that trusteth in Him. —Psalm 34:8 (KJV)

Little Sister, young and fair
How sweet it is for me to share
The wondrous joy that comes down from above
Listening with such delight
Desiring to do that which is right
Oh "taste and see that the Lord is good!"

The tears are welling in your eyes
Cause me to pause and wonder why
I felt you didn't care at all before
And, too, the tears from my eyes fall
Watching as you break down those walls
That hindered you from opening up the door

Oh Sister dear, do you too feel
That maybe Christ is someone real
Who wants so much for you to take His hand
Is there a yearning deep within
To be no longer bound by sin
And to have a hope that meets all life's demands

My God is real; I know it so!
He's with me everywhere I go
He gives me strength to live from day to day
Give Him the chance to prove to you
That He can give you life anew
And soothe the pain you find along the way

To me, dear Sis, you mean so much
And I truly desire for you to touch
With hands of faith the Robe of Calvary

You cannot make it on your own
And you never have to walk alone
My Christ shall satisfy your soul... abundantly!

(To my sister, Rose Mary)

July 23, 1979

How excellent is Thy lovingkindness, O God! therefore the children of men put their trust under the shadow of Thy wings. They shall be abundantly satisfied with the fatness of Thy house; and Thou shalt make them drink of the river of Thy pleasures. (Psalm 36:7–8, KJV)

Mother

To the world, you are a mother, but to your family, you are the world.
—Unknown

A master artist is pressed to paint
a portrait so wondrously fair
as hands embracing warmly
those beneath your care
The brushstrokes—though engaging
fail to blend the perfect tones
to capture the sweetness of your love
toward each of your own

A renowned author cannot express
in thoughts or fitting words to write
to convey the depths of emotions
in those long and restless nights
when your children were out in the world
or maybe a distance from home
and the numerous prayers you sent to God
to keep them safe and warm

Momma, I too fall short of words
to voice our regard for your tender care
and our gratitude for the love you've shown
throughout these challenging years
The full of all you are to us
only our Heavenly Father knows
for this Earth holds no such utterances
to express how we love you so

(To my mother, Thelma V. Riley)

July 27, 1979

As one whom his mother comforteth, so will I comfort you; and ye shall be comforted in Jerusalem. (Isaiah 66:13, KJV)

'Twas the Night after Thanksgiving

How very good and pleasant it is when kindred live together in unity!
—Psalm 133:1 (NRSV)

(A New Orleans Thanksgiving in Buffalo)

'Twas the night after Thanksgiving
When all through the house
The family was laughing
And running their mouths
The gumbo was stored in the 'frigerator with care
With plenty leftovers for the family to share

Momma, Roy and Cedric were all nestled in their beds
While visions of hot gumbo danced in their heads
And Myles and Nadia with Teetee in her lap
Had just settled down for a long winter's nap
When out of the kitchen there arose such a clatter
And Rosie jumped up! What was the matter!
Away to the kitchen she flew in a flash
Then all of a sudden, we heard a great gasp
For what to her wondering eyes should appear
But Benjamin lurking with a nervous blank stare
The dreaded dark shadow on the newly swept floor
And the light from the fridge revealed something more
With the smell of the spices her nostrils were filled
She knew at that moment the gumbo had spilled

More rapid than eagles the others they came
And looked all around for someone to blame
And Chris who was nodding now sprung in the air
And Delores at that instant stopped curling her hair
Beverly went breathless and started to choke
While Joslynn was laughing and thought it a joke

The gumbo was gone; we could hardly perceive it
Ben said he was sorry, but we didn't believe it
For he went back to chatting and laughing some more
As if our dear gumbo had not hit the floor
Yes, the gumbo was gone and indeed this was tragic
But who in the world would be the one to tell Cedric

When Ben finally decided to clean up the mess
We counted our losses, and we all had to laugh
For family is precious and is all that is dear
And there will surely be gumbo at Thanksgiving next year

Delores Riley Francois, Joslynn Francois-Hart
Beverly Riley Graves, Rose Mary Riley

November 24, 2012

(Adaptation from "The Night Before Christmas" by Clement Clarke Moore)

Warm Embrace

To every thing there is a season, and a time to every purpose under the heaven: A time to be born, and a time to die; a time to embrace, and a time to refrain from embracing. —Ecclesiastes 3:1–2, 5 (KJV)

It was such a warm embrace, Dad
you and I today
you held me close
as if you would never let me go
and though others were around
no one saw you here
and no one knew
that I was lost within your arms

Life is so very fragile
and some of the experiences
that add to the sum of our lives
often go unnoticed
and misunderstood
and then suddenly
our time is gone

And yet, every once in a great while
we are allowed the opportunity
to reach across the chasm of time
and venture back to a place where a little girl
can hold her father's hand
and look into his eyes
and smile

We were together again, Dad
at that special place
you and I
for within the arms of family
I found the memories you left for me
for my sisters, my brothers
my mother

I understand now
and I can say with tender sweet release:
"It is enough
that you loved me"

Yes, it was indeed a warm and strong embrace
I will carry it with me for always

Goodbye, Daddy—I love you

July 6, 2009

(Dedicated to my cousin, Sheila Crumbley)

Final Praise

Enter into His gates with thanksgiving, and into His courts with praise: be thankful unto Him, and bless His name. For the Lord is good; His mercy is everlasting; and His truth endureth to all generations. (Psalm 100:4–5, KJV)

Ever So Grateful!

Sing unto the Lord, all the Earth; shew forth from day to day His salvation. Declare His glory among the heathen; His marvelous works among all nations. For great is the Lord, and greatly to be praised: He also is to be feared above all gods. —1 Chronicles 16:23–25 (KJV)

Behind this written treasure trove
Of poetic words and verses
Stands the Majesty of Heaven
Whom against the night emerges
Displaying great His mighty works
Declares His glory among the heathen
For He that is feared above all gods
Is the Creator of Earth and Heaven

And Thou Sweet Lamb of Calvary
Hath shown to us salvation
O great and marvelous are Thy works
And unsearchable Thy creations
And I, who bows beneath Thy care
Doth hold Thy countenance beautiful
And pledge allegiance to His Grace
From a heart that is ever so grateful

For out of the depths of woeful night
My cries were heard and favored
And Thy merciful deliverances
Hath made Thy love most savored
O I proclaim Thy wondrous name
Jehovah God, My Savior Gracious
Keep me, Lord, as Thine one beloved
And my lips shall honor Thee with praises

O Thou for whom my soul adores
Bind me in weighted chains of gold
That I may ne'er escape Thy love
But upon Thy loveliness behold
Thou art My Sweet and Most Beloved
Who hath made my heart supremely full
Thus I, alone, remain of men...
Most blest and ever so grateful!

April 25, 2021

(Dedicated to My Sweet and Most Beloved)

Index of Titles

CPSIA information can be obtained
at www.ICGtesting.com
Printed in the USA
BVHW021102301121
622865BV00022B/1165

9 781956 896114